PROPHETIC FORECAST

VOLUME 3

DOUG ADDISON

Prophetic Forecast, *Volume 3*
By Doug Addison
Copyright © 2017 by Doug Addison

All Scripture quotations, unless otherwise indicated, are taken from the Holy Bible, New International Version®, NIV®. Copyright © 1973, 1978, 1984, 2011 by Biblica, Inc.™ Used by permission of Zondervan. All rights reserved worldwide. www.zondervan.com. The "NIV" and "New International Version" are trademarks registered in the United States Patent and Trademark Office by Biblica, Inc.™

Scripture quotations marked NKJV are taken from the New King James Version®. Copyright © 1982 by Thomas Nelson. Used by permission. All rights reserved.

Scripture quotations marked MSG are taken from *THE MESSAGE,* copyright © 1993, 1994, 1995, 1996, 2000, 2001, 2002 by Eugene H. Peterson. Used by permission of NavPress. All rights reserved. Represented by Tyndale House Publishers, Inc.

Scripture quotations marked TPT are taken from The Passion Translation®. Copyright © 2017 by BroadStreet Publishing® Group, LLC. Used by permission. All rights reserved. ThePassionTranslation.com.

Scripture quotations marked NLT are taken from the Holy Bible, New Living Translation, copyright © 1996, 2004, 2007, 2013, 2015 by Tyndale House Foundation. Used by permission of Tyndale House Publishers, Inc., Carol Stream, Illinois 60188. All rights reserved.

Printed in the USA

For ordering information contact:
InLight Connection +1 (805) 346-1122
PO Box 7049, Santa Maria, CA 93456
DougAddison.com

Cover Design by Seth Kellough

Book design by Treasure Image & Publishing
TreasureImagePublishing.com +1 (248) 403-8046

CONTENTS

ACKNOWLEDGMENTS

My biggest thank you goes to my wife Linda for her unending love and faithful support. She has been a great encouragement to me in the writing of this, as well as many other books. Several hours each day go into spending time with the Lord in order to capture the revelation that has been flowing.

I also want to thank the InLight Connection team for all of their work on this project—Krista Abbott, Arlene Brown, Dee Collins, Jenny Collins, Shannon Crowley, Seth Kellough, Joel Maust, and Diana Woods. Also thanks to Sherry Ward of SquareTree Publishing for editorial consult.

I am so appreciative to everyone for all of the hard work that was put into editing and preparing this project for release.

ENDORSEMENTS

Doug Addison is a revolutionary thinker. He's brilliant at helping us see outside the box and does it again in *Prophetic Forecast, Volume 3*. If you want to be inspired, get ahold of a copy now.

Shawn Bolz
Prophetic Speaker
Author of *Translating God* and *Keys to Heaven's Economy*
Exploring the Prophetic podcast

Doug Addison is one of the most gifted prophetic voices of our generation. His passionate message to demonstrate God's love to those who are still seeking is crucial to ushering in the next big move of God. Don't miss Doug's latest book, *Prophetic Forecast, Volume 3*, to find out what's coming next!

Wendy Griffith
The 700 Club Co-host

I strongly recommend Doug Addison's *Prophetic Forecast, Volume 3*. I am used to his forecasts being accurate and helpful, but this one had another level of anointing and impartation on it.

Doug experienced 50 days of "behind the veil" encounters and it is quite evident that this is from another level. It contains the keys for cooperating with the amazing Kingdom season we are in.

Johnny Enlow
International speaker
Author of *The Seven Mountain Prophecy,*
The Seven Mountain Mantle, and *Rainbow God*

Prophetic Forecast, Volume 3 is a must-read book for every Spirit-filled Christian. In this book Doug Addison shares his 50 days of supernatural encounters. Each one brings to light a fresh dynamic for the greatest harvest of souls.

I believe God revealed His heart for the harvest to Doug Addison through these 50 days of supernatural encounters. Readers should be wise and pay close attention to the words of this prophet. God has a plan and this book hits the target.

Bonnie Jones
Bob and Bonnie Jones Ministries

I highly recommend Doug Addison's new book *Prophetic Forecast, Volume 3,* which shares valuable insights into this new season.

If you need the Word of the Lord or a spiritual reality check, you need to make this new book part of your arsenal for the new season. In the pages of this book are incredible insights and revelation that will bring clarity and understanding for your life!

Jeff Jansen
Global Fire Ministries International
Author of *Glory Rising* and *Furious Sound of Glory*
Senior Leader of Global Fire Church & Global Connect

Doug Addison's *Prophetic Forecast, Volume 3* is a well of deep revelation, insight, teaching, wisdom and strategy. I know you will be as blessed by this *Prophetic Forecast* as I was.

Lana Vawser
International Speaker
Author of *Desperately Deep: Developing Deep Devotion and Dialogue with Jesus*

This book will open the eyes of your heart to the mysteries of God's Spirit, as well as reveal to you what's right around the corner prophetically.

I highly suggest this book to anybody who desires to see into Heaven or have encounters in God's glory, as it will inspire and impart an anointing to know God more.

Jerame Nelson
Speaker
Author of *Encountering Angels* and
Burning Ones: Calling Forth a Generation of Dread Champions

PERSONAL NOTE
FROM DOUG ADDISON

Before you begin, I have an encouragement for you and also a few things to be aware of. We found these out during the writing and editing process and wanted to pass them on to you.

The revelation in this book is not only *for* you, it is also *about* you.

As human beings, it is easy for us to read a book and see how it relates to other people. But I want to encourage you to make this book personal. As you read this, you will find treasures that God has in store for you and things He wants to speak to you. You might find yourself coming back to certain chapters and rereading them more than once.

You are called to be a part of this new move of God!

Whenever you find yourself reading this, trust that you have been set aside and prepared to be a part of what God is doing now. You may be a forerunner. You may have even been rejected or wounded by some Christians. And whether you are part of a church or not, this book is for all who want to say *yes* to the new things God is doing in the world.

I encourage you to ask the Lord to reveal to you what you need to see about yourself and your assignment in this new season.

Expect to encounter the presence of God in some way.

It's good to read this book, but it is even better to *experience* it.

Almost every person who set aside time to read a draft of this manuscript—especially the journal entries I have included from my heavenly encounters—has experienced feeling the presence of God. Some felt a heavy, weighty presence, while others started getting really tired all of sudden, like they needed to take a nap. Many experienced visions or received new insights or revelation from the Lord, too.

This happened to me several times while writing it. The weightiness of God's presence can be felt on this book and you might even feel it when you tell others about the encounters I will be sharing with you. Don't be surprised if your dream life changes and you start hearing the Holy Spirit speak to you throughout the day.

Whether you experience a tangible presence of God or not, the important part is to get what God is saying into your spirit so you can gain a better perspective of what God is doing and what is coming to you.

My prayer for you as you experience the revelation in *Prophetic Forecast, Volume 3* is that you would encounter Heaven in a deeper way and come into Heaven's timing and purposes for you here on Earth, so you can experience God's love for you in fresh, new ways.

Doug Addison

INTRODUCTION TO THE PROPHETIC FORECAST

I am the Lord; in its time I will do this swiftly. Isaiah 60:22b

The spiritual atmosphere is very ripe for something new. God is moving and preparing for a radical revival that will start first in our own lives. We have been in a dry season in which many people have not seen the fulfillment of prophetic words and promises from God. In the midst of what might look like conflicting prophetic messages, the Lord is indeed bringing His instructions.

I heard the Lord say, "Get ready for promotions and for things to start happening quickly this year." Many people have been waiting for God to move in their lives, and to bring a much-needed revival to the world.

Get ready for things to begin lining up like never before. Expect to hear the voice of God much more clearly, as you are being called up to a new level of breakthrough and maturity. God can speak to us in so many ways, but most people are not aware or have never had the proper training to discern it.

God speaks to me on a regular basis, and I journal every day to capture it all. I sometimes go through seasons of losing sleep as I get up early or stay up late when the Holy Spirit or angels are present and moving in my house or hotel room. At other times, the atmosphere can seem to dry up. We have to walk by faith, knowing that God is still present, even if we are not hearing His voice.

God is the God of love. He is not angry and He wants to draw people everywhere into a relationship with Him. Because the world is currently full of negativity and fear, we need to overcome these spirits by loving people and revealing the side of God that most people have not seen before.

If you read any prophetic words that invoke fear or anger, then there is a good chance it is not from the Spirit of the Lord. God is calling us to reconcile the world to Himself and we have our work cut out for us. We need to become like Holy Spirit *MASH units*.

Mobile Army Surgical Hospitals (MASH units) were set up on the front lines of war to save the lives of the wounded. We have our share of spiritually wounded people these days. Sadly, many Christians have become modern-day crusaders, thinking they need to *stand for the truth*, but they have done so at the expense of the ones who need God's love the most.

Using our beliefs to push people away from God is not what Jesus had in mind when He said the greatest commandment is to love (Matthew 22:37–40). This is why I am a positive prophet of love. In this book, I am going to open my heavenly journal to you so that you know what I am hearing from God and how I hear Him. I am doing this so you will know that God and Heaven are real!

Volumes of the Prophetic Forecast

Then the Lord replied: "Write down the revelation and make it plain on tablets so that a herald may run with it." Habakkuk 2:2

Most people know me from my *Daily Prophetic Words* and prophetic blogs that are shared on the internet. I also release monthly prophetic words on my *Spirit Connection* webcast and then distribute them through blogs and articles that go all over the world. Because I get such a large amount of revelation, it is sometimes a challenge to understand what is for now and what is for later.

A Note on This Series

This is Volume 3 of the *Prophetic Forecast* series I began publishing in 2016. I started writing the *Prophetic Forecast* series after two spiritual experiences with the Lord and an angel in 2015. Because I release so many prophetic words, they can easily be forgotten. The Lord gave me instructions on how to pull them together into books and volumes that will allow you to grab hold of what God is doing now.

After releasing the *Prophetic Forecast* books for 2016 and 2017, I realized some people were confused and thought the prophetic words in them were limited to that one particular year, when it was actually referring to the prophetic words I received to release that year. While they were released in 2016 and 2017, they are not limited to those years. For example, in my *2016 Prophetic Forecast* I released a 24-month revelation, which is starting to happen in 2018. So, these prophetic words lay a lot of the foundation and groundwork for what God is doing right now, and are still relevant words to read in the current season.

In order to clear up this misunderstanding, I have chosen to rename the *Prophetic Forecast* series by volume number, and no longer include the year in the title. *2016 Prophetic Forecast* is now *Prophetic Forecast, Volume 1* and *2017 Prophetic Forecast* is now *Prophetic Forecast, Volume 2*. If you have not already, I would highly recommend reading these previous volumes. And even if you have read them in the past, it would be a good idea to review them once more, as it will bring perspective on what God is doing now.

Special Time to Hear the Lord

Although I do not celebrate Jewish holidays, I do make myself available to listen to God's voice during particular times and seasons. The ten days between the Jewish New Year *(Rosh Hashanah)* and the Day of Atonement *(Yom Kippur)* are called the *Days of Awe.*

It is a time each year when God examines our lives for the purposes of promotion. Even though we are no longer under the Law of Moses, God still operates on the Jewish calendar as well as the Gregorian calendar (the one that most of us are familiar with).

Our Lives Are Examined Each Year

Historically, Jewish people believe that God examines our lives during the time between Rosh Hashanah and Yom Kippur to see if we are ready for spiritual advancement or promotion to a new level of maturity.

Whether you are aware of it or not, this is a time when you are able to hear God more clearly and gain direction.

Here is what is written about this time on Wikipedia.org:

"According to Jewish tradition, God inscribes each person's fate for the coming year into a book, the Book of

Life, on Rosh Hashanah, and waits until Yom Kippur to *seal* the verdict."[1]

God opens the Book of Life over all of us each year during the time of Rosh Hashanah, Yom Kippur and the Feast of Tabernacles. Here is a recap of the process that happens each year:

- God examines our lives during the Jewish New Year (Rosh Hashanah).

- Ten days later, on the Day of Atonement (Yom Kippur), He seals the verdicts regarding the assignments and possible promotions coming for the new year.

- God then reveals the results eleven days later, on the last day of the Feast of Tabernacles, also called Hoshanah Rabbah.

This is a total of 22 days. You can read more about these Jewish holidays in Leviticus 16; Leviticus 23:23–44; Numbers 29 and Deuteronomy 16:13–15. The time around the Days of Awe is important for your life because it prophetically sets the course for the upcoming year. Depending on when you read this, these dates may have passed for the year; nevertheless, something significant

---

[1] Wikipedia contributors. *Yom Kippur* [2.1 Heavenly Books are Opened] Wikipedia, The Free Encyclopedia. Retrieved from https://en.wikipedia.org.

happened for you in Heaven, even if you were not aware of it in your natural life.

Heavenly Books Opened

In Daniel 7:10, books (or scrolls) in Heaven are opened, and the Courts of Heaven review them. These books can be about us personally, as in Psalm 139:16, or about greater issues locally or globally. They contain blueprints and strategies needed to advance the Kingdom of God in our lives and on Earth.

From a prophetic standpoint, the Jewish New Year begins on the last day of Rosh Hashanah, which in 2017 was September 22nd. Most people, however, operate based on the Gregorian calendar, in which the New Year begins on January 1st of each year.

I am writing this book from the standpoint of both. Since most people are used to the Gregorian calendar, I release prophetic words on my blog for the year starting in January. I am writing this *Prophetic Forecast, Volume 3* based on what I heard God say to me during the Days of Awe of 2017.

Keep in mind that prophecy is intended for strengthening, encouraging, and comfort (1 Corinthians 14:3). Many people expect prophecy to be judgmental, but the New

Testament teaches us that the prophetic gifts function to build us up. They were not meant for "doomsday" material. So get ready to hear the voice of God and watch as things begin to open up for you.

Billion Soul Revival and Bob Jones

I learned most of what I am sharing with you—about God moving and speaking more clearly during the Days of Awe—from the late seer-prophet Bob Jones. The Lord visited Bob every year on Yom Kippur and gave detailed instructions and strategies for the coming year. Bob would release them in his annual *Shepherd's Rod* books. I had the opportunity to be mentored by Bob and Bonnie Jones and to speak with them at conferences and churches.

In order to understand many of the prophecies in this book, it helps to be familiar with some of Bob's major prophecies. I wrote about this with a deeper understanding and updated timeline to Bob Jones' prophecies in Chapter 3 of my *Prophetic Forecast, Volume 1*. I highly recommend reading this, as it will add context to what God is doing now.

On August 8, 1975, Bob Jones died and was taken into Heaven to meet Jesus. Instead of being invited in like the others who were in line with him, Jesus sent Bob back to Earth with a mandate to prepare the Church for a major revival—the revival of all revivals. The Lord told Bob that there would be a movement on the Earth that would bring in one billion people, and that the majority would be young people who were considered outcasts and offensive to the current Church.

This came to be known as the *Billion Soul Revival*, and Bob's entire life and ministry were centered around this prophecy. He was known as the "prophet of love," and he went back to Heaven on Valentine's Day—February 14, 2014. His passing occurred before he was able to see the start of the revival. But God has not forgotten this prophetic promise, and things are now lining up for it to come about.

My Connection to It All

I have been around the prophetic movement for many years. I spent the entire decade of the 1990s as a business owner, an undercover prophetic evangelist in San Francisco and a church planter. In 2001, God captured me with a powerful encounter and mandate. I had just been healed of Huntington's disease, so I left pastoring and sold my business to pursue a greater call on my life—though I was not yet sure what it was.

I watched a videotape of Bob Jones being interviewed by Wesley Campbell at a conference in Kelowna, British Columbia, Canada. The Holy Spirit came on both my wife and me with power. God spoke to me that I was being given an assignment to help Bob Jones fulfill his life calling for the Billion Soul Revival that was coming. It seemed far-fetched and impossible, but it was the Lord who spoke it!

I was literally out of ministry at the time, an unknown former pastor and business owner. At age 42, the Lord spoke to me to get ready and sell it all because He was about to move us into our destiny.

My wife and I had a huge yard sale. We sold everything except our personal belongings, moved into a tiny apartment in Burlingame, California, and waited on the Lord's instructions. Within three months, God gave us a plan.

We moved to New Hampshire, and Linda and I joined the staff of John Paul Jackson's Streams Ministries for a short time. Within a few months we met Bob Jones, and I got to share what God had spoken to me. We started our ministry, InLight Connection, in 2001 with the sole purpose of training people in the prophetic to help fulfill Bob's mandate of the Billion Soul Revival.

We moved back to California to pursue this vision. A few years later, we moved to Moravian Falls, North Carolina, and bought a small cabin where I began having angelic encounters.

During that time, I had the opportunity to be mentored by Bob at his house and to travel to conferences with him and his wife, Bonnie. As I look back, I have to pinch myself and say, "Is this a dream?" How amazing and faithful our God is!

I want to be clear that I am not saying I have the mantle of Bob Jones. What is coming is bigger than one man, woman or ministry can fulfill and we all have a part in it.

Special Visitations This Year

During the past year, I began having more encounters with the Lord—in various forms—than I have ever had in my life. Something opened up in the spiritual realm, and God began releasing greater measures of revelation and supernatural encounters.

This came in the midst of a great deal of turmoil on the Earth with the increase of violence, extreme weather, superstorms, earthquakes, floods and catastrophic fires. In the midst of this shaking going on around us, God is preparing for some amazing things coming over the next few years.

Revelation is flowing like never before! What God is speaking is flowing in such detail that I am not able to capture it all while typing—I had to start using dictation software on my computer in order to keep up! Since Passover 2017 (in April), I have had daily, 2–3 hour heavenly encounters. Most of it is about the coming Great Revival, as it is known in Heaven.

Many people were promoted spiritually this year. The Lord is now releasing special plans and assignments for those who have walked through the painful preparation it takes— the ones who cry out for mercy (and not judgment) for others (James 2:13).

And let us not grow weary while doing good, for in due season we shall reap if we do not lose heart. Galatians 6:9 NKJV

I heard the Lord say, "This is your due season, and it is overdue for many." Do not give up, as this is a season to reap. It is not far off. Things are going to begin lining up for you over the next few months. The Lord has not forgotten you! For many, the very reason you came to Earth is about to be revealed to you.

In this *Prophetic Forecast, Volume 3*, I have included several encounters from my heavenly journal. I have also included some prophetic words that I released previously because they are relevant to what God is doing now.

Keep in mind that God is outside of time, so these prophetic words are not limited to times and dates. The

Lord told me that when people read some of these encounters, they are going to activate and open the heavens over them. My prayer is that you encounter God's love and receive a radical breakthrough in your life.

CHAPTER 1

ENCOUNTERING HEAVEN

The veil between Heaven and Earth is now opening up more. God is preparing us for some amazing times of global revival, and He is getting us ready to receive and release prophetic mysteries from Heaven. These mysteries will expand our understanding of what is already written in the Bible and how it applies to our lives today.

The release of this new revelation is happening right now. God is opening up our understanding to things that were previously sealed, because they are needed for the time and season that we are now entering. This does not mean that we abandon the foundational teaching of our faith in Jesus Christ.

An example of this is found in the book of Acts. It was not until the coming of the Holy Spirit that the apostles began to more fully understand the Old Testament, or *Tanakh*. They suddenly saw Jesus and themselves in the ancient writings, and they also experienced supernatural encounters.

If we are not careful, we can read right over these New Testament experiences and not realize that God is still very supernatural—and these things can happen to you. All things are possible for those who believe (Mark 9:23).

I have become its servant by the commission God gave me to present to you the word of God in its fullness—the mystery that has been kept hidden for ages and generations, but is now disclosed to the Lord's people. Colossians 1:25–26

We are now in a season when our lives on Earth will change radically as we grow in our understanding of what Jesus meant when He said, "on Earth as it is in Heaven."

[Jesus said,] "This, then, is how you should pray: 'Our Father in heaven, hallowed be your name, your kingdom come, your will be done, on earth as it is in heaven.'" Matthew 6:9–10

Heaven is not just a place you go to when you die. It is much more than what we have seen on TV or in documentaries about people who have died and come back to life. Heaven is the place where God dwells; Jesus and the angels are there as well.

The Holy Spirit and messenger angels bring things from Heaven to Earth (Hebrews 1:14). We interact with Heaven physically and spiritually. We were created to live our lives connected daily to God, who is in Heaven.

The Glory of God Returned in March 2017

I released a prophecy in *Prophetic Forecast, Volume 2* concerning the return of God's glory to the church. During the Jesus People Movement in the early 1970s, there was a strong presence of God's glory. It was like a liquid anointing or tangible atmosphere that could be felt by many people. Without God's greater glory and power, we will not be able to be part of a revival and movement as big as what God has in store for us.

In 1975, the Lord spoke to the prophet Bob Jones that the greater glory of God was going to leave the Church, because it was used for man's gain instead of for revival and the Lord's work. On March 11, 1977, Bob saw this glory lift from the Church, and it did not return for 40 years. Yes, there have been people who still carried portions of it, but overall, the glory of God has not been on the Church at large since that time.

March 2017 was the 40th anniversary of the glory departing. I have to tell you; it was during that same week that I experienced the return of the glory of God—just as the Lord had spoken through Bob Jones. I was taken in a vision into Heaven and I interacted with the Lord. He began speaking to me about the coming revival with details and strategies.

Like the glory of the 1970s, it will not be limited to the four walls of a church. Similar to the Jesus People Movement, the glory of God is coming with signs and wonders, healing and miracles, and will begin to touch those outside the Church and pour into the streets.

That encounter was the start of something that has not stopped since. A little over two weeks later, on April 4 (4/4), I began 50 days of heavenly encounters.

50 Days behind a Veil

Starting around the Jewish holiday of Passover in 2017, I spent 50 days behind a veil that few people know about or have experienced. We read about it in the Bible, but do not realize that the spiritual, heavenly realm that is mentioned so often is actually real. We tend to think of Heaven as a place where we will go in the future when we die—but Heaven is a very real and relevant place. The Lord is interacting with us all the time, but it is concealed behind a veil. Once in a while, we may hear someone talk about encountering an angel or having a supernatural experience that cannot be explained.

Many Christians today have put God in a box, and most often experience Him only through reading the Bible or going to worship services. God is way bigger than these things alone. We tend to focus only on the healing miracles of Jesus Christ. But when I read the Bible, my eyes are continually opened to the awesome (and sometimes strange) occurrences that have been recorded for us.

We serve a God who cannot be explained. In the Bible, waters part, donkeys talk, thunder speaks, water turns to wine, angels perform prison breaks and earthquakes open prison doors. I have seen and experienced so many supernatural occurrences and miracles that I have lost count. I want you to know this amazing side of God, too.

Very truly I tell you, whoever believes in me will do the works I have been doing, and they will do even greater things than these, because I am going to the Father. John 14:12

Foundation for the Supernatural

The main principle and purpose of experiencing the supernatural is found in Ephesians 1:17. This is actually the banner over my life and ministry. I have built all of my life's work and ministry on this foundation:

I keep asking that the God of our Lord Jesus Christ, the glorious Father, may give you the Spirit of wisdom and revelation, so that you may know him better. Ephesians 1:17

Everything we do and all of our revelation and spiritual experiences are laid on the foundation of knowing God better. When it comes down to it, the things we need most of all are godly character, humility and love. That is a rock–solid foundation that you can build an amazing life and ministry on, and it can support the weight of all kinds of things. When we come into alignment with this, we can then step into a time in which all things are possible for the one who believes (Mark 9:23).

Love is the cornerstone of this foundation. Jesus said the greatest thing is to love others as He loves us. He reminds us through the apostle Paul that it all comes down to faith, hope and love—and the most important is love (1 Corinthians 13:13).

Heaven Opened

When all the people were being baptized, Jesus was baptized too. And as he was praying, heaven was opened and the Holy Spirit descended on him in bodily form like a dove. And a voice came from heaven: "You are my Son, whom I love; with you I am well pleased." Luke 3:21–22

Shortly after the baptism of Jesus and the heavens opening, Jesus prophesied to Nathaniel that he would see the heavens open and he would see angels:

He then added, "Very truly I tell you, you will see 'heaven open, and the angels of God ascending and descending on' the Son of Man." John 1:51

This is similar to the experience that Jacob had in Genesis 28. He saw Heaven open in a dream and the Lord spoke to him. The Bible is full of these types of encounters.

Once you understand how God speaks and how the Kingdom operates, you can actually live under an open heaven wherever you go. That means that you can stay connected with God spiritually so you hear and experience Him more clearly.

Jesus took His closest disciples—Peter, James and John—up on a mountain to pray, and the heavens opened before them:

After six days Jesus took with him Peter, James and John the brother of James, and led them up a high mountain by themselves. There he was transfigured before them. His face shone like the sun, and his clothes became as white as the light. Just then there appeared before them Moses and Elijah, talking with Jesus. Matthew 17:1–3

Wow! That must have been a radical encounter for them all. Peter, James and John got a glimpse into the heavenly realm that is around us all. Peter wrote that he was an eyewitness to this, and he encouraged us to stay grounded with the truth about Jesus and His majesty (2 Peter 1:16–18). This is another example of Heaven coming to Earth.

To experience the fullness of the love of God, we must not discount His supernatural side. I want to lay a foundation for just a few of the supernatural encounters in the Bible. Get ready, because this is a time and season that God is going to open the heavens over you. The Lord spoke to me and said many people are going to start experiencing more of the supernatural this year and in the times to come. All it takes is an open heart and spirit, and to ask the Lord for more of Him.

Opening the Spiritual Atmosphere

We can create an atmosphere of either faith or unbelief; one opens up the spiritual realm and the other closes off our supernatural connection with God. It is interesting to note that Jesus could not do miracles around an atmosphere of unbelief (Mark 6:5; Matthew 13:58).

In order to experience God and all that He wants to bring to each of us, we must start by believing that all things are possible! We must focus on the good things of God, not our failures or shortcomings. Did you know that you can have actually foster an atmosphere of unbelief, and that will close things down (Matthew 13:58)? Likewise, you can cultivate an atmosphere of faith and belief, which will open things up for you (Matthew 15:28; Luke 7:9). Many people are finding themselves in a spiritually closed-down mode.

It is so important for us all to live a lifestyle of gratitude, worship and faith, as opposed to regularly grumbling or complaining. It is the ungodly combination of unbelief, grumbling and complaining that can close the heavens over you. This can not only affect your ability to hear and experience God, it can also harm your health and even your finances.

We Have to Activate It

We must use the power of believing and having faith to start activating supernatural things. Then we can shift the atmosphere to the positive by applying biblical principles such as:

- What you sow is what you reap (Galatians 6:7)

- If you give, you will receive (Luke 6:38)

- If you believe, you will become (Luke 1:45)

- Judge not and you will not be judged (Matthew 7:1–3)

- Humble yourself and you will be lifted up (James 4:10; 1 Peter 5:6)

I am sure you are familiar with these amazing and powerful biblical principles. They are important, because if you begin to live them out instead of doubting and grumbling, then you will see positive changes in yourself and in the spiritual atmosphere around you.

Living as a Shadow of Heaven

These are a shadow of the things that were to come; the reality, however, is found in Christ. Colossians 2:17

We are actually living in a spiritual shadow or reflection of Heaven right now while we are on Earth. There are many teachings on types and shadows of the Jewish feasts and the temple.

The symbolism throughout the Old Testament is meant to show glimpses of God's Kingdom on Earth (Colossians 2:16–17; Hebrews 10:1). It shows how we are often living these things out every day as a shadow of what is happening in Heaven. That is where we take on the characteristics, the attributes and even the fragrance of the Lord and Heaven everywhere we go.

Supernatural Encounters in the Bible

There are many examples of what I call *heavenly encounters* in the Bible. Philip was taken in the spirit from one place on Earth to another (Acts 8). There are accounts of people being taken into Heaven, like Isaiah (Isaiah 6) and Elijah (2 Kings 2); the apostle Paul was also taken into Heaven and shown revelation (2 Corinthians 12:2). The book of Revelation is full of these translated-into-Heaven encounters, as well.

You can have an angelic encounter on Earth. An angel of the Lord suddenly appeared to Peter and—right then and there—freed him from prison (Acts 12:7). These were actual events that happened in the natural realm as a result of the angelic presence.

A more common way to have encounters with the Lord is through dreams and visions (Matthew 2:19–22; Matthew 27:19; Acts 16:9). We, too, can have encounters through these kinds of dreams and visions. They are different and greater than regular dreams.

There are accounts of people having a visitation from Jesus. In Acts 23:11, Jesus appeared to Paul and told him to go to Rome. If you read Acts 20–23, you will see that at first Paul sensed the Spirit saying something, then an angel stood in front of him, then Jesus appeared to him. It was all later confirmed by the prophet Agabus (Acts 21:10–11). Look at the process the apostle Paul went through before going to Rome and being put into prison. It was a high calling, so it required multiple and increasingly greater confirmations.

Learn to Discern

We need to practice hearing God, especially in the approaching season.

But solid food is for the mature, who by constant use have trained themselves to distinguish good from evil. Hebrews 5:14

Most people are not used to the idea of practicing hearing God's voice. But if you think about it, we practice all the other gifts to get better—things like preaching, teaching, singing, playing worship music and even organization and administration. Why not practice hearing the voice of God? This will help us deal with the fear of being deceived. Constant use of our spiritual gifts will fix this issue. Learn to discern, and you will not be duped!

Staying Grounded

When we are talking about the supernatural things of God, it is important to stay grounded in the Bible. We are not trying to change the truth of who Jesus is. We must build our spiritual lives on the foundation that Jesus is the Son of God and He died for our sins. He rose from the dead and ascended into Heaven according to the messianic prophecies from the Old Testament.

God has manifested Himself in three forms—the Father, Son and Holy Spirit—yet all are one God. There are angels of the Lord as well. We do not worship the angels or pray to them. We pray to God the Father, in the name (authority) of Jesus, and through the power of the Holy Spirit. We should always make our requests to God the

Father, and not try to contact angels or people who have died and are now in Heaven.

When God speaks to us or we experience something supernatural, it is important to ask the Lord for confirmation of it in the Bible. We need to test the spirits and all of our encounters (1 John 4:1–3). You will also benefit by writing down the things that God says to you. Journaling and recording what God is doing will help you advance to an entirely new level.

I want to lay a foundation for the supernatural so that you will better understand the experiences and prophetic words I am releasing in this book. Now let's go deep into what God is saying for the coming years. I have found that it is better not to limit these words to a specific date or time frame.

Sometimes things are for now and sometimes they are for later. God is not limited in time and it is important to view prophecy with this in mind. When we try to lock a prophetic word into a certain date or time, we can miss the broad brushstrokes the Creator is speaking to us.

CHAPTER 2

THE REJECTED REVIVAL
OF THE REJECTED ONES

You may have noticed that we have not had a revival or major move of God in North America for quite some time. As I have previously written in the *Prophetic Forecast* volumes, we had a revival or major move of God every 11 years or so until the 1990s.

If you follow the 11-year pattern from the 1906 Azusa Street Revival, you will notice that 11 years later, 1917, was the start of Aimee Semple McPherson's impact—later, the powerful 1950s Healing Movement. Moving forward, in the 1960s there was the Charismatic Renewal, and in the 1970s, the Jesus People Movement, followed by the Third Wave Charismatic Movement of the 1980s and the Toronto Blessing in 1994.

Since 1994, we have not seen a sustainable move of God's power or revival, although we did see an extension of the Toronto Blessing take place a couple of years later with the Brownsville Revival.

During this time, Bob Jones was alive and prophesying the Billion Soul Revival. I remember Bob saying that it was going to start after the population of the Earth reached 6 billion, as that is what Jesus told him in 1975. This milestone took place just before Bob Jones had a face-to-face encounter with Jesus while in Redding, California, on February 28, 2001.

The Lord told Bob that there would be a movement that would reinstate the prophetic and be geared toward young people. Bob was a seer-prophet and would refer to the Billion Soul Revival as *building a spiritual house* for the youth. My wife and I watched a videotape in 2001, in which Bob Jones was talking about this. In that same year, we launched InLight Connection to fulfill this prophecy.

Bob prophesied that a movement among the spiritual outcasts would start within a few years. The 11-year interval I mentioned would have put the start of that movement at 2005. At that time, I was traveling and training people in prophetic evangelism, expecting this to happen.

Sadly, instead of a revival of the radical outcasts and young people, many of them were pushed away by Christians. After interacting with tens of thousands of people in the streets—over a decade of doing prophetic evangelism outreaches—we got a similar response from the people we were trying to reach. They were not asking if God was real, they were asking why Christians were so mean to them.

I was so shocked at the levels of rejection that people were experiencing. My *apologetics* quickly turned into *apologizing* and asking forgiveness, trying to bring healing to them. As I tell you this, I am not bitter or angry at the Church. In fact, I am still a pastor and my ministry, InLight Connection, is an internet church.

A Rejected Revival of Rejected People

On April 10, 2007, I received a phone call from Bob Jones. He told me about a spiritual experience in which he was given a paid receipt from Heaven to buy the lumber to build the "house" for the Billion Soul Revival. In the experience, Bob went into a lumberyard and placed the order from Heaven on the counter, but the foreman refused to fill the order. Bob picked up a silver hammer that was lying there, pounded it on the counter and demanded the goods, but the foreman refused, so Bob left.

Bob told me that the foreman was not a demon, but represented many leaders and people in the Church at that time. He said that the Billion Soul Revival is made up of a new radical group of outcasts that God wants to draw in, but they are offensive to many Christians.

This new revival that is coming will be raw and messy, but the current Church is more comfortable with reaching out to people that seem safer to them. Bob's health declined after this, and he died seven years later in 2014. At that time, many Christians may not have realized that they had said "no" to this next move of God. Now it is time to pick up the calling and bring it into reality.

Burnt Stones

Ironically, the revival for the rejected and wounded people was actually rejected by many Christians. As a church planter, my wife and I geared our church startups toward this group of people. It was not easy, as many of them were known as *burnt stones*—that is, people who were wounded and did not fit into other churches.

Other pastors and even my church-planting overseers told me to beware of the burnt stones. They tended to show up at new church plants, because they did not fit in (and were rejected by) other churches that may not have understood them. Many of these wonderful people were often uncomfortably beautiful. The Lord loves these people, and when Jesus came He hung out with a similar crowd.

Somehow, we must have had extra grace and a calling from God to reach these outcasts. Our first church plant in

1998 had its share of rejected burnt stones, but we created a safe place for people to heal and be accepted by God's love and to experience His power. A church is not a building, but it is made up of people. So, when I heard Bob Jones talk about building a house for the revival, I understood that he meant it would be done with people, and not so much the organization that we are used to in churches today. Please understand that I am not judging Christians or churches, and I believe we need all types of churches to reach all types of people.

Cornerstone and Capstone

A *cornerstone* is an architectural term for the first stone that is placed in the foundation of a building; for a stable structure, all the other foundation stones must line up with the cornerstone. A *capstone* is placed at the top of an arch or doorway, or as the roof of a building, and is often the final stone put in place. The Lord is constructing a spiritual building laid on the foundation of the apostles and prophets from the Bible, and Jesus is the cornerstone.

Consequently, you are no longer foreigners and strangers, but fellow citizens with God's people and also members of his household, built on the foundation of the apostles and prophets, with Christ Jesus himself as the chief cornerstone. In him the whole building is joined together and rises to become a holy temple in the Lord. And in him you too are being built

together to become a dwelling in which God lives by his Spirit.
Ephesians 2:19–22

This spiritual building God is constructing is made of people, not just a church building or organization. I have had several dreams, visions and spiritual experiences in which I have seen this new spiritual building. It will house the coming revival and it is not a physical building. Bob Jones used to refer to this as the *house* for the Billion Soul Revival. This spiritual house, or revival, has been rejected for generations. Many of you reading this right now are called to be part of this new spiritual building. And just like Jesus, you may have experienced rejection.

The Living Stone and a Chosen People

As you come to him, the living Stone—rejected by humans but chosen by God and precious to him—you also, like living stones, are being built into a spiritual house to be a holy priesthood, offering spiritual sacrifices acceptable to God through Jesus Christ. For in Scripture it says: "See, I lay a stone in Zion, a chosen and precious cornerstone, and the one who trusts in him will never be put to shame."

Now to you who believe, this stone is precious. But to those who do not believe, "The stone the builders rejected has become the cornerstone," and, "A stone that causes people to stumble and a rock that makes them fall." 1 Peter 2:4–8a

Revival of the Rejected

If you study the history of revival, you will find that many of the revivalists we hold in high esteem from the past actually suffered a great deal of rejection from the established Church of their day.

This is common. Jesus Himself was rejected by the majority of people, especially religious leaders—even His hometown. That said, we can all expect some degree of rejection for carrying the message of Jesus.

When God releases a major movement or revival, it is because we are in need of change. We have stopped reaching people and have not been effective in winning people to Christ for the past few decades. Studies indicate that many children who grow up going to church never return after they come of age.

Yet somehow, many Christians began to reject people who need the Lord. This often includes their own children who are in lifestyles that they disagree with. There are many groups of people that are no longer accepted or treated kindly by Christians because of their orientation, lifestyle, political views and in some cases their race and gender.

Heavenly Encounter: The Stones Others Rejected

This encounter is from my heavenly journal. It happened on May 3, 2017. In this encounter, the Lord was speaking to everyone, not just me. Quite often, this is the way that the Lord speaks to me. I live out prophetic words in my life, and I report to others what I experience. I get a lot of feedback from others about how accurate these experiences are, and I have learned over the years to share them for encouragement, comfort and direction.

Heavenly Encounter: May 3, 2017

Most all of the spiritual encounters I have involve the Lord directing me to a place in the Bible. As I read it, I begin to have visions and they are quite real and detailed. Though I am not physically there, I can sometimes smell, taste and feel things as if they were real. On this day, the Lord directed me to Psalm 118.

The stone which the builders rejected has become the chief cornerstone. This was the Lord's doing; it is marvelous in our eyes. Psalm 118:22–23 NKJV

[Beginning of Encounter]

Suddenly, I was taken to a place in the spirit that I cannot describe, except that I was there. I was sitting with others, and the Lord was speaking to us.

The Lord said, "You (referring to all of us) are the cornerstone that the builders from previous generations have rejected. This is the new Great Revival of the outcasts that many people have been rejecting for many years. And people have rejected you over this as well."

I could now see there was a very large stone that had the words written on it, *The Great Revival.*

The Lord said, "The stone the builders rejected has become the capstone that many of My people, prophets and leaders have rejected. But you have cried out for it day after day and gave your life, even in the face of death. When you began to cry out for this, Satan sent all that he had to try to stop you and your generation. But you did not give up crying out day and night for this revival to come. You did not back down, though the attacks against you were sometimes beyond what you could bear."

Decree from Heaven

Then what looked like a video screen opened and a vision appeared in midair of many people praying Psalm 132. This was something I had been praying almost daily to the Lord for the past few years—for the Billion Soul Revival to come.

Lord, remember David and all his self-denial. He swore an oath to the Lord, he made a vow to the Mighty One of Jacob: "I will not enter my house or go to my bed, I will allow no sleep to my eyes or slumber to my eyelids, till I find a place for the Lord, a dwelling for the Mighty One of Jacob." Psalm 132:1–5

The Lord spoke these words as He looked us in the eyes, "Today I have remembered your self-denial. And today, I am issuing a decree from Heaven that the time has now come for the fulfillment of all that you have cried out for. The time has now come for repayment for all that you have lost, crying out for The Great Revival to come to the Ezekiel 34 weak sheep and the Billion Soul Harvest that other prophets gave their life for."

Then the Lord unrolled the golden scroll and read these words from Psalm 2:7–8: "I proclaim this decree: 'You are My son; today I have become your Father. Ask Me, and I will make the nations your inheritance, the ends of the Earth your possession.'"

This was not just for men, but also for women. God was making a decree to the sons and daughters who have been crying out to Him day and night. This is the time for us to enter into our spiritual inheritance. The very purpose and reason we were born and came into the world is now going to unfold.

The Lord said, "You have asked for revival and gave your lives for it. So, this day I decree that all you have asked for in My name will now come to pass."

As the Lord spoke these words, we fell down before Him and began to worship. I was overcome with His power and presence, and was getting an impartation of His unfailing love for people. Being this close to the Lord was like being next to a liquid waterfall of love and warmth. It was like sunshine and refreshing water all at the same time. Nothing else seemed to matter, and our focus was on Him.

The Great Revival Stone

We began to worship the Lord and give thanks for all that He had done for us. Then the Lord invited us to stand on the stone marked *The Great Revival*. It was a very large, smooth, rectangular-shaped platform. As I stood on it and next to many others, I felt very protected and grounded in the Lord. I could feel the mind of the Lord suddenly open up, and I began to understand His heart for this new revival that is coming.

I could suddenly see those who are still in darkness, but whose names have been prepared for the Lamb's Book of Life. These are the ones who were rejected over the last few decades. This is the Billion Soul Harvest and the Ezekiel 34 lost sheep. I could hear them crying out, "O Lord, save us!"

I fell down on the stone I was standing on and cried. I wept bitterly and said, "Lord, don't hold back any longer. Send Your workers into the harvest field and open up the gate for salvation, that these people may enter."

I looked up at the Lord, Who was still holding the decree that said I could ask for whatever I wanted. Then He held His hands up and said, "Let this be done on Earth as it is in Heaven, as this is my Father's will."

A New Gate Opened

Then I saw a golden gate open that had been previously shut. This was the Psalm 118 Gate of the Righteous that led to salvation. From this gate, the workers of the harvest and the gathering angels began to pour in. I could see the workers begin to assemble. These were the ones who have been called to be part of this new move of God. They were the ones who had a spiritual mark on them and had been set aside for this time. The workers were assembling and the wind of the Lord begin to blow upon them, and they were being revived. They were crying out, "Lord send us! Lord send us for the harvest has now come!"

One angel standing there spoke more words from Psalm 118: "This is the gate of the Lord through which the righteous may enter. And this is the stone other builders rejected but it is now becoming the chief capstone. For the Lord has done this and it is marvelous in our eyes."

I knew that the stone represented the coming Great Revival. And the fact that it became the chief capstone means that is now God's priority. We all knew that the gate that opened was the gate through which those who had been rejected by many Christians could now come into salvation. I am not sure what happened after that because there was a lot of worship and activity being released. Preparations were now underway, and I knew that we would start to see things happen quickly.

[End of Encounter]

What Are You Waiting For?

God is opening a new gate for those who have been waiting to be released into their destiny. This is a time to call out to the Lord and ask Him to open opportunities for you. Possibly, you have felt held back, rejected or even forgotten by the Lord. This is the time for you to come into agreement with the Lord's plans. Get ready to move forward, as things are going to start happening quickly.

CHAPTER 3

REVIVAL OF THE SONS AND DAUGHTERS

More from My Heavenly Journal

During the 50 days of supernatural encounters I had, the Lord gave me detailed instructions and strategies about the coming revival. The Lord told me I was going to have 49 days of heavenly encounters, and then the 50th day would be a celebration. This happened during April and May of 2017. As I explained in previous chapters, these encounters were in the form of detailed interactive visions. The Lord would open a section of the Bible to me and as I read it, I was taken into a heavenly vision that is hard to describe. It was so real and detailed that I had to use dictation software to capture it all.

As a seer-prophet, I often have visions and have to look things up in the Bible afterwards as a confirmation. But these encounters were different. I was taken to the Bible first, then I would have the visions. The Lord did this so that I (and others reading this) would understand and know it is grounded in the Word of God. The Lord spoke to me that the 49 days of encounters represented Isaiah 49, which contains a great deal of revelation about the coming revival.

In the previous chapter, I shared an encounter from my heavenly journal on May 3, 2017: The Stones Others Rejected. I would recommend reading all of Chapter 2 first, if you have not already done so. It will lay the foundation and context for what I am going to share in this chapter. I want to go deeper with this and share an encounter I had a few days later, on May 7.

Setting the Stage

I have been a pastor and an outreach specialist for several decades. As a prophet, I specialize in prophetic evangelism and was one of the forerunners for using prophecy and dream interpretation as a means of reaching people with God's love. For example, I am sometimes known as *The Tattoo Prophet* even though I do not have any tattoos myself. It started years ago when I began using Holy Spirit-led prophetic words to interpret tattoos because a billion people have tattoos and piercings!

Please note that the Lord is speaking some very straightforward words about those who have rejected people who need His love. This is not saying that all Christians are bad or have done these things. I am not being negative or judgmental toward the Church, and I believe we need churches to reach people. I am praying that you have an open heart to hear the words of the Lord for those He is calling.

The Great Revival is coming, and it is going to be for the forgotten ones. Many of them are tattooed and pierced, LGBTQ, into New Age, and even zombie and vampire lovers, to name a few. Yes, these might very well be our own sons and daughters who may not be interested in church or Jesus right now. The Lord is saving the best for last, and we are being invited to be part of it! Now that you know my heart, let me open my heavenly journal with you once more.

Heavenly Encounter: May 7, 2017

I was awakened at 4:00 a.m. with anticipation because the Lord has been speaking to me in great detail over the past few weeks. I am really excited for what is coming today! My *Daily Prophetic Word* for May 7, 2017: "Old ways will not work for you, so ask God to show you the new and what to do with it."

God has been speaking to me about strategies we will need for the coming revival. To respond to my *Daily*

Prophetic Word that said, "old ways will not work," I asked the Lord, "Show me the new ways that You have for us and what to do with them." I had dreams all night in which I was interacting with the Lord, having to do with John 3. I did not understand the details of it, but I knew that God was imparting new revelation to me about bringing people to Jesus and about His love.

The Holy Spirit took me to several sections of the Bible that I knew were going to be part of the encounter I was about to have. I bookmarked them in my Bible, and I began to pray in the spirit. I recommend opening your Bible right now to put bookmarks in John 3; Malachi 3–4; Luke 1 and Isaiah 49. What I am about to share with you is going to open up revelation that you may not have seen before. Since I do not have space in this book to include these chapters of the Bible, it is a very important part of the process to at least have your Bible open to these verses.

[Beginning of Encounter]

Met with the Lord

Around 5:30 a.m., I was taken into a detailed vision and I met with the Lord. I was wondering, "What are we going to do today?" The Lord was sitting comfortably in a chair and motioned for me to sit in the chair next to Him. There was a small table between us that might have had some documents or books on it.

The Lord said, "I want to give you deeper revelation about the dreams you had last night regarding John 3. My people understand John 3:16—that I have come into the world to save it. But they have not understood John 3:17, *God did not send his Son into the world to judge and condemn the world, but to be its Savior and rescue it!* (TPT).

"The Father sent Me into the world to love it and not condemn it. I was sent to save it, and I brought light into the world, and it was the light of love. Many of My people have rejected love and have kept the light for themselves. Yes, many of My people are rejecting and condemning people instead of loving and accepting them. I want to reveal some things to you that are coming. I want to give you understanding into the condition of things and My plans for the coming revival."

Not Just Tithes Being Robbed

Then the Lord spoke to me about the prophecies from Malachi 3 and 4. The Lord said, "Your land is under a curse, but it is not from robbing Me of your tithes like many are saying (Malachi 3:8).

"Many of My people have not understood Malachi 3, where I say that I will come like a refiner's fire and a launderer's soap. I have come near to My people to cleanse them of their deceptive ways.

"'So I will come near to you for judgment. I will be quick to testify against sorcerers, adulterers and perjurers, against those who defraud laborers of their wages, who oppress the widows and the fatherless, and deprive aliens of justice, but do not fear me,' says the Lord Almighty (Malachi 3:5).

"My Church has an abundance of adulterers, and those who are dishonest and defrauding, and have oppressed the fatherless and deprived people of justice. Yet they judge others for their sins, and this has opened the door to Jezebel and the operation of Christian witchcraft, which is sorcery. Many of them have not cared for the spiritual widows and the orphans, and most of all 'the fatherless.' The fatherless are the sons and daughters that have been abandoned. These are the lost sheep that have been cast away.

"It is not tithes that my people are guilty of robbing Me of. It is the injustice of not loving those I have called you to reach: See, I will send you the prophet Elijah before the great and dreadful day of the Lord comes. He will turn the hearts of the fathers to their children, and the hearts of the children to their fathers, or else I will come and strike the land with a curse (Malachi 4:5–6).

"My people have rejected their call to bring the spirit of Elijah, and they have rejected the sons and daughters. This is why your land is under a curse. It is not because of the lack of tithes; it is from not understanding your call to love and bring justice to the oppressed and fatherless.

"The cries of injustice from the fatherless—your sons and daughters and those rejected by My people—have reached My ears. I must now respond to their cries saying that they have been forgotten. This is why injustice is being exposed in your land. But those who have listened to Me and loved the people that I have called them to reach have now been marked to be part of this new Great Revival that is coming. Their names are also in a scroll of remembrance (Malachi 3:16). They have been set aside to help lead this coming Great Revival."

Understanding the Spirit of Elijah

Jesus said, "You must understand the spirit of Elijah and the words spoken by the angel about John the Baptist:

"And he will go on before the Lord, in the spirit and power of Elijah, to turn the hearts of the parents to their children and the disobedient to the wisdom of the righteous—to make ready a people prepared for the Lord." Luke 1:17

The Lord said, "Your generation is called to go before Me with the spirit and the power of Elijah to turn the hearts of the fathers to the children and the disobedient to the wisdom of righteousness. This will prepare My people for what is coming. The disobedient people that Luke was referring to were not those who did not believe in Me, but it is My people who have been disobedient with their calling to love their sons and daughters in the spirit of Elijah. This is why the Great Revival is coming to the sons and daughters and those who have been rejected by My people."

Lost Your Voice to the World

The Lord continued, "Zechariah did not believe the words of the angel, Gabriel, and he lost his voice (Luke 1:20). It is the same with My people who have not believed the prophets and those I have sent to tell them about the coming revival. As a result, My people have lost their voice to the world, and no one comes to churches to hear My voice like they have in the past.

"They did not believe my servant, Bob Jones, who proclaimed for 40 years the coming revival will be in the youth. They became jealous and wanted the revival to come through their generation and not on the young people. Their own sons and daughters had the invitation to bring revival, but many of them were pushed away and told they could not worship Me because they were tattooed and pierced, gay and lesbian, and lovers of zombies and vampires. These are the outcasts, and the very ones I love and died for.

"It was an injustice for My servant, Bob Jones, to proclaim his message with power and signs that followed, and yet My people rejected him. He came back to Heaven without seeing the fulfillment of the prophecy of the One Billion Soul Revival. Even now, My people have forgotten his words, and the words of many other prophets, who proclaimed the coming revival.

"Just as Elizabeth was in seclusion and was a disgrace among the people for her call to bear John the Baptist, so it is with you and those who have been called to prepare My people for what is coming. You will suffer disgrace with the people but, like Elizabeth, you will be shown great favor by Me" (Luke 1:25).

Preparation and Plans

After hearing these words, my eyes are suddenly opened wide to the condition of the Church, our country and the world. Many of the Lord's leaders have used Malachi 3 to get people to give money, which is okay to do, but they have failed to see that it also speaks about extending justice and love. We are now under a curse for rejecting those the Lord sent us to reach. I felt the heavy hand of the Lord upon me, and I fell down weeping. I asked the Lord, "Is there anything we can do to break this curse and to prepare the people?"

The Lord said, "The day that a postage stamp went up to forty-nine cents (January 26, 2016, in the U.S.) was the day that I began doing a new work in the world to prepare for the coming Great Revival. I am now moving on you and bringing the words from Isaiah 49 to reconcile many of the lost sons and daughters, and the Ezekiel 34 lost and abandoned sheep. Many of you have overcome much and have been faithful to do all that I've told you to do."

The Isaiah 49 Gathering

" ... I will not forget you! See, I have engraved you on the palms of my hands; your walls are ever before me. Your children hasten back, and those who laid you waste depart from you. Lift up your eyes and look around; all your children gather and come to you. As surely as I live," declares the Lord, "you will wear them all as ornaments; you will put them on, like a bride." Isaiah 49:15b–18

Suddenly there was a multitude of people surrounding the Lord. I knew it was those who had been crying out for revival and had been set aside for special assignments. I could tell these people had been through the wilderness and difficult times. Many of them were crying out words and prayers from Isaiah 49. I heard many yelling, "Lord, don't forget us! Please don't forget us!"

Then the Lord began praying words from Isaiah 49. As He did this, our names were inserted, and we could all hear the Lord speak our names simultaneously. The Lord said, "Before you were born, I called you from birth and I made mention of your name. I made your mouth like a sharpened arrow, and I have hidden you in the shadow of My hand. I have made you into a polished arrow and concealed you in My quiver. You are My servant, and I will display My splendor through you."

The group that had gathered around the Lord said, "But Lord, it feels like we've labored with no purpose and spent our strength in vain—for nothing."

The Lord said, "I formed you from your mother's womb to be My servant and to gather the lost sheep to Me. I am now going to honor you and give you new strength. I am going to make you a light to the lost sheep and those that were rejected. In the time of My favor, I am now answering you. This is the day of your salvation, and I'm going to make you a covenant for the people and restore the land. I am reassigning desolate inheritances. These are the mantles and callings that have been cast aside or forgotten. I am sending you to the captives to say, 'Come out of darkness and be free!'"

At this point, the Isaiah 49 people suddenly gathered, jumped to their feet, and new strength and fire came into them. They began to shout and praise the Lord. They burst forth in songs, and a rumbling began that shook something open in the spiritual realm. Angels began to gather because of all the excitement.

... I will contend with those who contend with you, and your children I will save. Isaiah 49:25b

Then suddenly we saw the multitude of those who have been cast into darkness. We were surrounded by them, and the Lord said, "These are the billion souls I have called you to reach." We were all on a platform in the middle, surrounded by those in darkness. We could hear their cries. Some of them had small lights left in them, but most of them were in total darkness.

See, I have engraved you on the palms of my hands ... Isaiah 49:16a

The Lord held out the palms of His hands, and we could see the names of the billion souls appearing in gold and silver. All the names were flashing as Jesus held the palms of His hands out. The light that glistened off of the names began to reflect out into the crowd in darkness. Jesus was standing in the middle, and the names of those called to be reached looked like golden tattoos. As those in darkness saw this, they began to cheer. Jesus held up His hands, and new hope and life came into them. Jesus was smiling and laughing, and all of us on the platform were laughing and smiling and rejoicing as well.

The Lord looked at those of us on the platform and said, "The time of My favor has now come to you."

Afflicted Ones Will Arise

The Lord spoke these words from Isaiah 49:8–9:

"In the time of my favor I will answer you, and in the day of salvation I will help you; I will keep you and will make you to be a covenant for the people, to restore the land and to reassign its desolate inheritances, to say to the captives, 'Come out,' and to those in darkness, 'Be free!'"

Then angels ascended from Heaven and surrounded us. They began to sing songs in the spirit from Isaiah 49:13.

Shout for joy, you heavens; rejoice, you earth; burst into song, you mountains! For the Lord comforts his people and will have compassion on his afflicted ones.

Now all of us were joining the angels and singing the new song for the afflicted ones. And even those in darkness, those who are part of the afflicted and forgotten ones, were now getting an impartation of new hope!

[End of Encounter]

I came out of the encounter shaken. I wept before the Lord and, at the same time, I was happy and rejoicing. The heavy weight of the Lord's presence was on me, and I had trouble going about my day. Every time I read or share this with others, they feel the presence and weightiness of Heaven as well. Let the presence of the Lord wash over you as you are being prepared for something totally new. We are now going to enter into a season promised to us.

CHAPTER 4

THE PROMISED
SEASON IS HERE

Entering a Promised Season

And it shall be that if you earnestly obey My commandments which I command you today, to love the Lord your God and serve Him with all your heart and with all your soul, then I will give you the rain for your land in its season, the early rain and the latter rain, that you may gather in your grain, your new wine, and your oil.
Deuteronomy 11:13–14 NKJV

This is being fulfilled over many people right now. God is opening up repayment for suffering in the past. He is also fulfilling promises that have been spoken over you long ago. Expect to see the rain from Heaven, new wine and oil—representing the Holy Spirit renewing your life.

"On the day when I act," says the Lord Almighty, "they will be my treasured possession. I will spare them, just as a father has compassion and spares his son who serves him. And you

will again see the distinction between the righteous and the wicked, between those who serve God and those who do not." Malachi 3:17–18

The change that is coming will cause those who love others to be promoted to new levels. Loving is God's greatest commandment, and His love is a gift we can give and receive. Many have abandoned love and have allowed hatred to enter their hearts. God is going to bring a change and release new levels of His love for people.

What to Expect

God is revealing things to you that will be important because it is a time of realignment for the coming revival. God is moving on people who have been wounded or rejected by Christianity or are considered outcasts by the current Church.

There are over a billion people who are ripe and ready for this new move. God is looking for people to lay it all down, just like the early disciples laid down their nets, businesses and families to follow Jesus.

God is going to move on people who are willing to step away from older methods that are no longer effective and step into new strategies now coming from Heaven.

New Revival—Not Revival of the Old

See, I am doing a new thing! Now it springs up; do you not perceive it? I am making a way in the wilderness and streams in the wasteland. Isaiah 43:19

God is releasing something totally new from Heaven. We are about to experience an amazing revival that has been prophesied for decades. Many prophets have been seeing a radical revival coming that will be similar to the Jesus People Movement of the 1970s. This movement was offensive to the Church and many Christians of that time.

Over one billion people are on the list to be reached by this revival. It will require love and grace to reach those who have been wounded and driven away from God or deeper into darkness. God is love, and Jesus said that the greatest commandment is to love.

If I have the gift of prophecy and can fathom all mysteries and all knowledge, and if I have a faith that can move mountains, but do not have love, I am nothing. 1 Corinthians 13:2

Beware of the recent rise in negativity and being judgmental. Demonic forces of violence and division have been released on the Earth in the past year. This is exactly opposite of what God is about to release. Satan often opposes and tries to stop revivals and moves of God before they come. This has been going on around the world, as a sudden surge of anger and revenge has entered the hearts of many people. But God's plan is to release a revival of love and grace.

Strategy for the Coming Revival

The Lord has a strategy coming that will bring revival and renewal to many people all over the Earth.

This is what the Lord my God says: "Shepherd the flock marked for slaughter." Zechariah 11:4

The next revival is coming to those who have been forgotten, mistreated or neglected—instead of loved. Many of God's people have gone away from the very commandment that Jesus said is the greatest of all—to love. When we are not loving toward those who are doing things that are opposite of what we believe, then we may be pushing them deeper into darkness.

Love is an amazing gift and, somehow, we have misplaced it. We have to be careful not to let our beliefs, and our quest for holiness and doctrinal purity, divide us from those who need God's love and our acceptance of them as people.

Compromising the Truth?

When I share my message of loving people, the common response is that I'm compromising the truth. This is far from what I am doing. Truth without love is not love at all. If we stand for the truth without considering a person's ability to receive what we are saying, then we might as well be a noisy gong or a clanging cymbal (1 Corinthians 13:1).

We need to be careful that we are not pushing people further away from God by trying to stand up for what we believe. It is not about what we believe, but it is about a person understanding God's love for them. We must demonstrate the unconditional love of Jesus. He never forced Himself or His opinion on people. Instead, He stooped down and was willing to associate with people from all walks of life.

Humble yourselves, therefore, under God's mighty hand, that he may lift you up in due time. 1 Peter 5:6

The humility the Lord is referring to is your ability to love others and place your own opinion on hold when needed. Have you heard that God will never force Himself on anyone because of free will? Then why are God's people trying to force their opinions on others?

Shaking Happening

Therefore, since we are receiving a kingdom that cannot be shaken, let us be thankful, and so worship God acceptably with reverence and awe, for our "God is a consuming fire." Hebrews 12:28–29

God is also shaking things so that your foundation will be firmly established, and you will be able to handle the new levels and anointing that are coming to you. This is not intended to harm you, but to strengthen and prepare you for some amazing things ahead! Do not look at the storm, but keep your eyes on what is coming!

The shaking we are seeing in the world are birth pains for the coming revival. It is also the Lord shaking the world, including the Church, so that what cannot be shaken will remain. He is calling us to step away from fear and step into His perfect love. He is calling us away from divisions and into unity in the Spirit.

You will hear of wars and rumors of wars, but see to it that you are not alarmed. Such things must happen, but the end is still to come. Nation will rise against nation, and kingdom against kingdom. There will be famines and earthquakes in various places. All these are the beginning of birth pains. Matthew 24:6–8

These words spoken by Jesus are a direct reference to what is happening in the world right now. This is not saying that this is going to result in the end times and the great tribulation that many are preaching.

We are seeing catastrophic events of biblical proportions. This is a time to be encouraged because, after the shaking, a Great Revival is going to come—greater than anything we have seen. Get ready for the greatest show on Earth to begin.

Because of the increase of wickedness, the love of most will grow cold, but the one who stands firm to the end will be saved. And this gospel of the kingdom will be preached in the whole world as a testimony to all nations, and then the end will come. Matthew 24:12–14

Complaining Can Create a Whirlwind

I want to encourage you to not be afraid or worry about how things look. God is still in charge, and He is not causing tragedies and difficult times. They are coming from the enemy, who wants to distract us from the coming revival and great blessings.

Yes, these are difficult times, but stay in prayer and worship, focus on God and refrain from complaining and being fearful. Things are going to shift for you very soon.

Though you probe my heart, though you examine me at night and test me, you will find that I have planned no evil; my mouth has not transgressed. Psalm 17:3

We need to be very careful how we speak, because the Lord is examining our lives right now for the purpose of promotion. It is important to step away from speaking anything that brings division or lacks love and encouragement. I asked God why we are seeing such fierce storms, shaking and violence. He told me that it has to do with the negative whirlwind that is alive and active in the hearts of many people right now. It is also delaying revival and closing the heavens for blessings.

They sow the wind and reap the whirlwind. The stalk has no head; it will produce no flour. Were it to yield grain, foreigners would swallow it up. Hosea 8:7

The Lord said, "My people are complaining and sowing anger and taking up causes that are their own and not Mine. They are coming into agreement with the voice of the accuser, and with the spirit and fruit of darkness. I have called you to speak words of life. This is why there are such violent outbreaks all around the world, and also why the revival and harvest has not taken place."

In Hosea 8:7, the Hebrew word for wind is *rûach*, which can be translated as anger. Many people have been sowing anger, frustration, rebellion and revenge. This spirit is now trying to take over in the hearts of many Christians who have an assignment to carry the words of the Spirit—love and life—and not the words of the angry wind.

Gaining Authority in Prayer

God is calling us away from idle arguments and divisions, and to focus our efforts on His agenda and the things that matter most. This is a time to rally together in intercession and bless people we do not agree with.

We must love our enemies and pray for those we feel are persecuting us or our beliefs. This includes political and social justice causes, as well as religious and spiritual. There is power in agreement.

But I tell you, love your enemies and pray for those who persecute you. Matthew 5:44

Many people have lost their authority in prayer because they are coming into agreement with the accuser of our brothers and sisters (Revelation 12:10). I want you to do a check in your life right now: What is the fruit you are seeing in your life? Are you seeing answered prayers, financial blessings, people coming to the Lord or people coming to you to hear His wisdom? Or are you seeing the opposite?

If you are experiencing the latter, then there is a good chance you need to shift your focus to God's agenda, and not complain and argue with others over your cause or opinion.

Transfer of Wealth Coming

This next revival will require a lot of finances. Because of the tragedies happening all over the world, we need resources and money for humanitarian purposes. We will also need to finance some of the largest revival meetings we have ever seen. The outcasts we are called to reach may not have much money. These meetings will not look like what we currently see inside of the Church. I have seen glimpses of them in my interactions with Heaven, and I do not know exactly what it will look like—except it will be strange and geared toward people who the current Church may not accept.

This is all the more reason we will need finances! God said that He is now answering prayers that many Christians have been praying for years:

… the wealth of the sinner is stored up for the righteous. Proverbs 13:22b NKJV

Many people have been praying this prayer, not realizing that the Lord is trying to answer it. But first He must rid us of anything that is in the same spirit as the world.

God is now shaking things in our lives, our families, our businesses and churches. He is doing this to get our attention and cause us to focus on the business of God's Kingdom, not on the world around us. This is why there is such great shaking happening everywhere. But do not be afraid or discouraged. God is still in control and has a plan.

Be Humble and Repent

We are seeing a release of God's justice and judgment now coming all over the Earth. God is revealing things that people have done against others. The books in Heaven are being reconciled for injustices, and those who have been dishonest or mistreated people will be held accountable.

What you have said in the dark will be heard in the daylight, and what you have whispered in the ear in the inner rooms will be proclaimed from the roofs. Luke 12:3

This is why we are seeing injustices and scandals exposed. This is a time to be humble and repent for anything in our own lives before we speak out in judgment against others. Dishonest deeds are being exposed everywhere because God is calling us to a new level, and it will require honesty. Be sure to repent and bring matters under the Blood of Jesus, and things will be okay for you.

Call for Unity in the Spirit

Be completely humble and gentle; be patient, bearing with one another in love. Make every effort to keep the unity of the Spirit through the bond of peace. Ephesians 4:2–3

Changing the spiritual atmosphere will require us to let go of negativity and arguments. It is really important that we become one in the Spirit. Divisions are bringing disunity, which is allowing the enemy to attack us. A house divided against itself will not stand (Mark 3:25). Make every effort to restore the bond of peace and love for one another. God is raising up peacemakers that are being sent out to bring healing in the land. As this happens, we will see a change in weather patterns, a reduction of violent acts and the release of God's blessings on the Earth.

How to Respond

Devote yourselves to prayer, being watchful and thankful. Colossians 4:2

The spiritual atmosphere is now changing. What would have taken many people a lifetime to achieve will be accomplished in a short time. God is going to start moving radically in your life. It will help to stay focused, watch and pray. I cannot stress enough the importance of staying out of negative arguments and idle talk, especially on the internet.

The spiritual principle of *what you sow is what you reap* is very active right now. What we speak with our mouths can have consequences. We need to be careful and thoughtful with our speech. It is very important to sow love and unity in the Spirit. This will shift the spiritual atmosphere over you and those around you.

CHAPTER 5

TREASURY ROOM AND JOSEPH ANOINTING

Wealth without Understanding

This is from my heavenly journal, and was part of my 50 days of encounters in 2017. The Lord led me to Psalm 49, which is about having money and riches:

People who have wealth but lack understanding are like the beasts that perish. Psalm 49:20

During my quiet time the Lord spoke to me. He said, "I'm about to release wealth to people to help finance the coming Great Revival. Many have perished when I have done this in the past. This is because they lacked understanding and wisdom about how to handle wealth. It will be important to keep your eyes on Me and listen to My Holy Spirit each day, and not get caught up in the worry of money, as I will take care of you. I am blessing many people so that you can be a blessing to the generation that lost their inheritance. I am raising up the revival of the outcasts who do not have a lot of money."

Heavenly Encounter with Wisdom

The Holy Spirit directed me to Proverbs 9, "Invitation of Wisdom":

Wisdom has built her house; she has set up its seven pillars. She has prepared her meat and mixed her wine; she has also set her table.

She has sent out her servants, and she calls from the highest point of the city, "Let all who are simple come to my house!"

To those who have no sense she says, "Come, eat my food and drink the wine I have mixed. Leave your simple ways and you will live; walk in the way of insight." Proverbs 9:1–6

The fear of the Lord is the beginning of wisdom, and knowledge of the Holy One is understanding. For through wisdom your days will be many, and years will be added to your life. Proverbs 9:10–11

[Beginning of Encounter]

As I read through these verses, I began having visions of them and they came alive in the spirit. The Lord invited me into this experience. I was taken into the house in Heaven where I meet with the Lord each day. He was sitting in a chair as other times. There was an empty chair next to Him, and I sat in it.

The Lord said, "Today there are invitations going out to many people to enter the House of Wisdom. I want to take you into her house and let you meet Wisdom for yourself."

House of Wisdom

The Lord led me to the House of Wisdom. I entered in and saw a woman sitting there. She was very beautiful. She had long dark hair and very deep eyes that reminded me of the eyes of Jesus. There was a golden glow about her, and I could feel the presence of the Lord. The room had no lights except the light of the Lord coming from her. I sensed the light of life flowing from her, and it was an awesome experience.

I said to Wisdom, "I have lacked understanding and wisdom. I have often not understood what to do and acted out of my own thinking. I need your understanding." Wisdom said to me, "You will know my voice because of the peace that it brings. My voice is low and not loud. The proud are loud and haughty and have many words. But Wisdom has learned to speak only that which the Father is doing."

As I sat next to Wisdom, she did not say a lot of words. I thought she would give me advice and wise sayings. Instead she sat there in what looked like a rocking chair. As she rocked, she was in time with Heaven. She knew when to stop and when to rock. She knew when to speak and when to get up. She knew when to eat or drink and when not to. I realized that she had understanding that I needed. This had to do with the harmony of Heaven I experienced in a previous encounter.

Wisdom said, "Your suffering has brought you into understanding the fear of the Lord. You would not be able to cross the threshold of my house without this. Come and sit and eat with me." I sat down in a chair next to her, and there was a table between the two of us. On the small table between us was the Book of Wisdom. I thought I was going to eat from this book because there was no other food there, and yesterday in an encounter I was given books to eat (Ezekiel 3:3).

Key to the Treasury Room

We sat there for a long time, and Wisdom did not say anything. I felt very comfortable sitting in silence with her as I felt the peace of the Lord there. Then Wisdom said to me, "As you walk in my ways, fear the Lord and ask for understanding. This will bring light to your path. This will open up doors that have been closed. I am not giving you a Book of Wisdom today, but I am giving you a key. Then Wisdom handed me a golden key and said, "This key will open the door that is called the Treasury Room of Heaven."

I was wondering if there was a test in this. I came into the House of Wisdom thinking I would get a book or understanding of what to do. Instead I got a key to the Treasury Room of Heaven? Where was this room? Then Wisdom pointed to a door that was behind her. This was the doorway to the treasuries of Heaven—and I had the key. I asked permission to open the door, and she nodded. I stood up and walked toward the door. My feet began to burn with the anointing of the Lord, and my hand was warm from the key. I placed the key in the door, and it opened.

Inside the Treasury Room

I will give you hidden treasures, riches stored in secret places, so that you may know that I am the Lord, the God of Israel, who summons you by name. Isaiah 45:3

Inside, the room was extremely bright and golden. I stood at the threshold, not entering in as it took me a few minutes for my eyes to adjust from the brightness and be able to see. The Treasury Room of Heaven seemed to be a busy place, and it did not seem to be about gold, wealth or money. It was not about possessions; but it was all about understanding, wisdom and sound judgment.

I stood at the threshold of the door for what seemed like a long time, just allowing this golden light of the Lord to saturate my spirit man. Then I stepped inside the Treasury Room of Heaven and saw a door and hallway that led to another room, called the Riches of His Glory (Ephesians 3:16).

Wisdom was next to me as I ventured toward the door to the Riches of His Glory. As I stepped into this room, I understood suffering was just as powerful as blessing. I also felt strengthened as I stepped into this room.

I realized that the Treasury Room of Heaven could be accessed from different ways. There were people coming in through doorways with their family names on them, which were generational inheritances and blessings. Others were coming in through doorways marked Suffering for the Gospel. Others were coming in because they had been granted access for assignments they have received from the Lord. But I entered in through the Door of Wisdom that came from the House of Wisdom. This seemed to be significant, as it granted me greater access to other places.

Treasury Room Jail

I saw a large room with golden bars like a jail, and it was full of people who seemed to be waiting for something. I asked Wisdom, "How is it possible to be in jail in Heaven?"

Wisdom replied, "They are not in jail like you think of jail on Earth. This is a spiritual holding place for those with great callings, and they still have access to all that they need in Heaven. But their calling is not fully released yet. Many of them did not understand the Lord's timing, and others are waiting to be released with their life purpose."

I remembered in a recent encounter that I was shown the harmony of Heaven. Once we get into the flow of the Lord, then many doors will open to us. I realized that getting into the flow of Heaven would free these servants who still have callings for Kingdom finances and wealth.

Sadly, many of the people here seemed to be in the jail for life because they lacked understanding on riches and finances. I knew this meant that many of them who had life callings and prophetic words over them about having wealth may never receive it on Earth.

Joseph Anointing People Getting Ready

Also in this jail room were many prominent business people and servants of the Lord who had *Joseph Anointing* written on their shirts. I knew that these were the ones who, like Joseph in Genesis 40, were being held in reserve for a future movement and purpose of God. There seemed to be movement with this group.

Then an angel came in and began to single out many of the Joseph Anointing people. They were lining up as if they were going to be released. There was a doorway from this jail called Released.

At that doorway was a desk and angels giving assignments when it was their time to be released to bring this anointing from Heaven to Earth.

Word about Wealth

Wisdom turned to me and said, "You are about to come into wealth. It is both your generational calling and because you have suffered. It's a combination of repayment and provision for you. Your calling is great and you have suffered, so you can now be trusted with riches from Heaven as well as riches on Earth. Do not let wealth sway you from your calling. The wealth you are about to receive is to fulfill your calling. This is why you entered into the Treasury Room of Heaven through my house called Wisdom. You will need wisdom to handle the riches coming to you for the Great Revival."

New Assignments for Joseph People

Then an angel was standing next to me with a list of assignments that I thought were for me, but I was told they are for others. I thought the assignments would be on scrolls or parchment paper like I have seen in Heaven before. But these assignments were on what appeared to be high-tech pads or devices that I have never seen on Earth. The angel handed me these assignments, and told me that I was being given understanding and revelation to help coach and release Kingdom finances into the world.

Each of these assignments had the name of a Joseph Anointing person attached to them. Many of them were the least likely people on Earth. Some of them were not professing Christians, but loved the Lord and had an assignment from Heaven on their lives. Some of them were in the business world; some were in the entertainment industry. The angel said, "The Lord is going to use this unlikely group of people to release finances on the Earth for the purposes of the revivals that are coming."

Anointed as a Steward of Kingdom Wealth

All of a sudden, many angels gathered around me. Wisdom was still standing next to me. Then Jesus stepped up, and they all laid hands on me and gave me this new anointing of wisdom and revelation to unlock the riches of the Kingdom. I knew this was not just financial, but it was also wisdom and revelation to release finances, through plans and strategies, from Heaven to Earth.

Then I was given a scroll to eat. It was a combination of high-tech and ancient-looking at the same time: one side was an ancient scroll; on the other side were vibrant, hologram-type colors coming out of it because it was opened. It was placed in me and the Lord said, "I'm anointing you this day to be a steward of financial wealth."

I looked around, and I was not the only one there getting this. The Lord was anointing stewards of Kingdom wealth and imparting assignments for riches and revelation. Every time I heard the words *riches and revelation*, it also sounded like *revelation for riches*. One side of the scroll was revelation, and the other, high-tech side was the actual plans and strategies on how to bring it about on Earth.

Golden Mark of Favor

Then an angel was standing there and asked me to hold out my right arm. He touched my right bicep, and I could feel strength and understanding enter me. As his hand went away, a golden emblem or marking was left on me. I could not make out the details of it, but it was a marking from Heaven and was similar to a heavenly tattoo. I looked, and everyone getting this impartation and promotion today was getting marked. I was told that this mark will draw the right people to us at the right time. This was the mark of favor of the Lord.

Liquid Gold

Then the Lord asked me to stick out my tongue, and He poured what looked like liquid gold into my mouth. He said, "These are the words you will need. They will come to you at the right time, and you will not have to think about it."

The liquid in my mouth was very sweet and became thick and heavy as it went into me. My spirit man suddenly felt very heavy. I was feeling the weight of Heaven pressing upon me. I heard a voice say, "This weight is for those who have waited." It had something to do with understanding timing.

I looked down, and there were angels that looked like children painting my fingernails gold. They were rubbing something on me that was softening the areas that had become calloused because of my pain and suffering. Then a tall angel standing there reached into the bucket the children angels were using. He took a handful and thrust it into my heart. Suddenly my heart was softened, and I did not even realize that I had been calloused. He also placed it on my eyes and in my ears. I was being bathed in this liquid love, and I lost track of time. Then suddenly all the angels went to another person standing near me. They began doing the same thing to them that was done to me.

You Are Now Ready

The Lord said to me, "Son, now you are prepared to walk this journey. This is the race that you are called to run, and you are now ready to enter into a final season." I heard Him laugh and say, "This is the grand finale. It is not the end, but it is the beginning. I have saved the best for last. My blessings are on you and many in your generation."

I saw a doorway opening up for many people who were being promoted in the Treasury Room. Many of them were going out rejoicing and singing. It looked like a "fire tunnel of ministry" we sometimes do at churches on Earth. The angels were lining up on the sides, as well as people from their cloud of witnesses and generational fathers and mothers. It was a heavenly fire tunnel of blessing as these people were released back on the Earth.

I thought I was going to go into that line, but I was asked to take a seat for a moment and rest. There seemed to be some shuffling happening in the room. I realized that seven of us had been singled out from those who had just been promoted, and we were now assembling to receive something else. There were only a few people in this line, and I was halfway back from the front. I watched as people from their generational line came with special gifts. Each one seemed to be unique for them and their calling.

Billion Soul Platform Opened

Then it was my turn, and I stepped up on what seemed like a platform. And suddenly I was no longer in the room, but it was a platform to the world. Though I was still in Heaven, I could see what looked like a sea of people that I was going to reach for Jesus. It was 360 degrees around the platform, and they were all in darkness, but were lighting lights like candles.

There were others on the platform as well. As I stood on the platform, I could hear the cries of the people. Their lights had almost gone out. In fact, some of them had no light at all and were there almost in a dead state. But a billion people were crying out things like: "Come and save us. Don't forget about us," and the voices kept screaming for help over and over. It was terrorizing to hear their pain, and I was wondering where the Lord was.

Then the Lord Jesus stepped onto the platform with us. Suddenly everything lit up, and the people were no longer in darkness. They all had bright light radiating from them, and their cries of mourning and pain turned to rejoicing and celebration. Jesus looked at those of us on the platform and said, "Your suffering has now come to an end, and you are now going to enter into the reason you came to Earth."

Fire Tunnel in Heaven

Then a silver walkway appeared. The fire tunnel of angels and my cloud of witnesses were all cheering for me as I walked through. They were blessing me, imparting things to me, and all jumping up and down with joy. There was so much laughter and celebration happening as I passed through. Some of them handed me things that I would need. I was also given assignments and gifts they were not able to fulfill. Then I went into a bright light and came back to Earth at 7:34 a.m. ... I knew the time on the clock was significant, and the Lord spoke to me:

He looked up to heaven and with a deep sigh said to him, "Ephphatha!" (which means "Be opened!"). Mark 7:34

[End of Encounter]

Activating This over You

This encounter happened and involved me, but you need to understand that this is happening to you and many others all the time. Whether you know it or not, the Lord is anointing you to be part of what is coming on the Earth. Heaven is very real, and not just a place we go when we die. The Lord is very interactive with us all the time.

Get ready for the reason you came to the Earth to be revealed to you. The Lord is speaking these words over you and your situation, "Ephphatha! Be opened!"

CHAPTER 6

IMPARTATION OF HOPE

Now hope does not disappoint, because the love of God has been poured out in our hearts by the Holy Spirit who was given to us. Romans 5:5 NKJV

God is going to give you an impartation of new hope as you begin to see prayers answered and prophetic words fulfilled in your life. Watch for answers to forgotten prayers to start coming.

Many answers to prayers were delayed or caught up because of circumstances, people and the interference of the enemy. But now the heavens are opening up, and answers are going to start coming to you. They might look different than you expected, but watch for this to happen.

Many people have been through a difficult time, and now those who have survived the testing that preceded promotion are going to come forward.

On March 31, 2017, I awakened to a sound coming from Heaven. I heard it repeating over and over for about an hour. It seemed to come from shouts of praise and celebration.

God spoke to me that there is great celebration happening in Heaven right now because many people survived the testing and are now being promoted. This will become clearer, and the very reason you were created is about to be revealed to you!

Revelation Flowing during Passover!

Unrelenting disappointment leaves you heartsick, but a sudden good break can turn life around. Proverbs 13:12 MSG

If you have had prophetic disappointments in which God has spoken to you, but you have not seen things come to pass, then this is going to be a special time for you.

God is going to heal hope deferred and unrelenting disappointments. God is going to heal broken hearts and give sudden breakthroughs and life turnarounds.

Watch for this to come each year around the time of Passover, the Jewish festival that celebrates God's greatness to save when He gave instructions to the Israelites in Egypt that caused the disaster to "pass over" their houses (Exodus 11–12).

The prophetic aspect of Passover is still available to us today. When uncertain times come in the form of economic, spiritual, environmental or personal attacks against your family, health or finances, God can reveal strategies that will allow you to avoid them or even receive a blessing in the midst of difficult times (Genesis 26:12; Genesis 41).

God is going to release prophetic strategies for you during the time of Passover. They may come in the form of prophetic words, dreams, or God speaking to you through the Bible or other people. Be ready to hear the Lord more clearly and to receive revelation through dreams, visions and supernatural encounters. The heavens are open right now to hear God like never before. We are all going to cross over into a new season of victory and promotion!

Power Coming at Pentecost

The Jewish festival of *Shavuot* is more commonly known as Pentecost, and takes place 7 weeks (50 days) after Passover. Pentecost signifies the wheat harvest in Israel and the celebration of God giving the Torah to Moses on Mount Sinai.

During Pentecost, we will begin to reap what we have sown (wheat harvest) and God will give us His words as He did for the Israelites when giving the Torah.

Pentecost is also the day that the power of the Holy Spirit came upon the Church. Jesus was resurrected from the dead on Passover, and 50 days later the promise and power of the Holy Spirit came upon the early Church at Pentecost (Acts 2). This is a season of joy, power and revelation flowing to you from Heaven!

The people walking in darkness have seen a great light; on those living in the land of deep darkness a light has dawned. You have enlarged the nation and increased their joy; they rejoice before you as people rejoice at the harvest, as warriors rejoice when dividing the plunder. Isaiah 9:2–3

Gate Called Joy

I had an encounter with the Lord on Pentecost, May 31, 2017. This prophetic word is not limited to any date. I noticed that many of the prophecies and things God has spoken over seasons like Passover and Pentecost are not limited in time. This is because God is outside of time, and He can bring about these things in your life right now.

The Lord said, "It is Pentecost, and I am releasing revelation and power to My people who have suffered. New joy is going to come and replace your suffering. This is the time of the harvest in Israel.

"In the same way, you are going to reap a harvest for things you have sown in past seasons. At the end of the seven weeks of Pentecost, you will look back and say, 'I am in a new place.' Watch for Me to move in unusual ways and through circumstances that you might not understand at first. But stand on this word that I'm giving right now. In seven weeks, things are going to look different and new joy is going to overcome you." As the Lord spoke this, I was shown a new gate beginning to open in the spiritual realm. The name on the gate is Joy.

Heavenly Encounter: "Mother's Day Every Day"

On the morning of Mother's Day 2017, I had several visions of something special happening in Heaven.

[Beginning of Encounter]

The Lord said, "This is the day that you honor mothers on Earth, but I tell you mothers are honored every day in Heaven. Their purposes in life are often misunderstood, as the things they do appear to be humble and hidden. But in Heaven, their actions and prayers are very powerful. The prayers of a righteous woman are powerful and effective."

Prayers of Mothers and Women

Jesus pointed toward a section in Heaven that was dedicated to the prayers of mothers and women. I saw their prayers come before the Lord, and angels were assigned to their requests. I noticed that not all of the prayers were from biological mothers, but also from spiritual mothers. In Heaven it did not matter if you bore a child physically; the same honor was given to the spiritual mothers as was given to the physical mothers.

I watched as the prayers of women on Earth went into Heaven, and angels were capturing them. Some angels were scribes and captured them in books. Others were angels on assignment who had authority to release answers and resources. There were angels turning some of the prayers into songs that were being sung during this process.

You've kept track of all my wandering and my weeping. You've stored my many tears in your bottle—not one will be lost. For they are all recorded in your book of remembrance. Psalm 56:8 TPT

Books of Remembrance Reconciled

I saw shelves of books that had the recorded prayers of women and mothers. They lined the walls and went for eternity. These were the Books of Remembrance of the prayers that had not been answered. There were millions of books of unanswered prayers being brought before the Lord. I was thinking it would take a very long time to answer them all. The Lord stood up and raised His hands. Then suddenly, millions of angels came, and each took a book and carried it to a section of Heaven that had to do with that person's life and calling.

The Lord said, "Watch for the answers to these prayers to start coming, but it might look differently than what you might have expected."

Promotions of Women

Jesus said, "Many women have sown in tears, and they are about to reap a harvest of joy. Many are now being promoted with new authority, and spiritual gifts are coming to them."

I saw an angel holding a golden scroll. The angel began to read from the scroll the names of women being promoted. The scroll looked small but as the angel read, it kept going and going.

The Lord said, "These are the names of the women who are receiving honor in Heaven, and they are about to receive favor and blessings on Earth."

I watched as each name was read and an angel was dispatched to that person on Earth. The women were receiving blessings, repayment, new anointing and spiritual gifts. Some of them had not been recognized on Earth, even though they had done amazing things for the Lord.

Men Promoted and New Teams Formed

I was wondering, "What about the prayers and promotions of men?"

The Lord spoke to me that there will be many men promoted into new positions of authority each year on Father's Day, just as He did with women on Mother's Day.

I was told that this is just one section of Heaven dedicated to the prayers of mothers and women. There is another section with the prayers and promotions of men. The Lord chose Mother's Day to release to women these promotions and answers to their prayers.

[End of Encounter]

New Divine Alliances Coming

As God is bringing the promotions to women and men, I saw new partnerships and teams being formed—as both men and women are being promoted and being given new spiritual gifts, it is going to form new divine alliances. These are divinely orchestrated partnerships in ministry, marriage and business.

Two are better than one, because they have a good return for their labor. Ecclesiastes 4:9

God is bringing both men and women together to form strategic teams that will greatly impact the Kingdom. There will be a new unity in the spirit that will open up new ministries and businesses focused on doing God's will. This is going to align us for the coming revival.

Get ready for new joy as God is answering your prayers!

Father's Day Encounter

I had an encounter with the Lord on Father's Day 2017 in which God said that He is now releasing greater revelation and details about your eternal purpose and destiny. Please note that these encounters are not limited to time or specific dates, as God is outside of time.

The Lord is going to show you hidden things that have been holding you back in the past. On Father's Day, God said that He is going to reveal Himself to you as a father does to a son or daughter.

I will reveal the eternal purpose of God. For he has decreed over me, "You are my favored Son. And as your Father I have crowned you as my King Eternal. Today I became your Father. Ask me to give you the nations and I will do it, and they shall become your legacy. Your domain will stretch to the ends of the earth." Psalm 2:7–8 TPT

I also like the way the end of verse seven is written in the NIV—it says, "... *today I have become your father.*"

God is healing negative understandings and wounded hearts of fathers. Not all fathers on Earth were able to give or express the love of the Father. This is not to judge them, but the Lord is going to heal father-heart issues in our lives.

[Beginning of Encounter]

Chains and Contracts

In the encounter, I had a vision that an angel came with silver keys and unlocked chains that were on people. As the angel unlocked the chains, I saw another angel holding a stack of contracts and agreements that had been made with these restraints.

These had been placed on people by those who did not understand them or had become jealous. The chains and contracts had been holding these people back from moving forward in many areas of their lives. Most people did not realize they had these restraints. They had gotten used to operating within the limits that had been placed upon them.

... having canceled the charge of our legal indebtedness, which stood against us and condemned us; he has taken it away, nailing it to the cross. And having disarmed the powers

and authorities, he made a public spectacle of them, triumphing over them by the cross. Colossians 2:14–15

God said, "I am removing these chains, and I am now removing the contracts and agreements that were made with each one. I am disarming the attacks against you."

I saw the angel with the contracts take them to a blazing altar off in the distance. The contracts and agreements that have held you back in the past were burned up in the fire of the Lord.

As this was going on, new freedom was being released in the spirit. People's eyes were suddenly opening to things that happened long ago—things they came into agreement with or that needed to be broken off. As the new freedom came, they began to rejoice and worship God.

New Gates Open in the Spirit

Shouts of joy and victory resound in the tents of the righteous: "The Lord's right hand has done mighty things! The Lord's right hand is lifted high; the Lord's right hand has done mighty things!" I will not die but live, and will proclaim what the Lord has done. Psalm 118:15–17

Their shouts of joy and victory caused discouragement to fall off. Some had become so distressed, they were at the point of giving up and wanting God to take them to Heaven.

Others were suffering with suicidal thoughts. But these were all being broken!

I watched as many people began to shout and worship God. Then God stood up and raised His hands and said with a loud voice, "Open the Gates of Righteousness!"

Open for me the gates of the righteous; I will enter and give thanks to the Lord. This is the gate of the Lord through which the righteous may enter. Psalm 118:19–20

God said, "I will fulfill all the promises I made to you. The things I have spoken to you are now coming. I am now freeing you from the chains that have held you back. I am aligning you for this new season of your life. Stay close to Me and watch Me move in the midst of the storms.

"This is the gate for you and others, who are now entering into the season for which you were created. This is the Gate of Righteousness for those who prepare themselves. This is the pathway to My presence that will take you deeper into My intimacy and love. This is the way of My heart."

Those Rejected Now Accepted

The stone the builders rejected has become the cornerstone; the Lord has done this, and it is marvelous in our eyes. Psalm 118:22–23

I saw many people who were being freed from the chains and restraints of the past now flowing through this new Gate of Righteousness. They were given new freedom and purpose, and their strength was returning. Many of them had been rejected because they did not fit in. But now God is gathering the misfits and those rejected, and is building them into something new.

[End of Encounter]

I have experienced these things in my own life. As I have shared this with others, I have received lots of feedback about chains of the past being broken and new revelation coming. This is an exciting time as God is preparing us for the coming Great Revival.

Release of the Prisoners of Hope

Come back to the place of safety, all you prisoners who still have hope! I promise this very day that I will repay two blessings for each of your troubles. Zechariah 9:12 NLT

God has hidden many people away in prison, like Joseph in Genesis 41. Joseph was released suddenly and repaid for all his pain and suffering. The prison was not a fun place to be, but it was a place of hope and safety to him as he waited for the fulfillment of the dreams God had given to him as a child (Genesis 37). God spoke to me that He is beginning to call forth the prisoners of hope.

This is a time to press into the Lord in prayer and get ready for your marching orders that are coming. God is going to start releasing the prisoners of hope. He is going to bring new hope and use you to bring hope to people in need of His love. So, get your hopes up because you are going to be repaid double for all your trouble!

CHAPTER 7

TRIALS AND TEARS WILL BE WORTH IT

Consider it pure joy, my brothers and sisters, whenever you face trials of many kinds, because you know that the testing of your faith produces perseverance. Let perseverance finish its work so that you may be mature and complete, not lacking anything. James 1:2–4

Trials Will Bring Advancement

It will be important to not resist or run from the trials and testings that are happening now. Testing is not a bad thing, and God is going to use it to prepare you for the advancements and promotions that are happening (and will continue). We are in a time of the Lord's fire coming to test our works.

Their work will be shown for what it is, because the Day will bring it to light. It will be revealed with fire, and the fire will test the quality of each person's work. If what

has been built survives, the builder will receive a reward.
1 Corinthians 3:13–14

Speaking Positively Matters

New power and authority are coming upon your words. You will need to be careful what you say, because your words can be spiritual life or death. They can build up and tear down—especially in the season we are now entering. There are many spiritual principles that can open the heavens over you or close them off.

Seeing a fig tree by the road, he went up to it but found nothing on it except leaves. Then he said to it, "May you never bear fruit again!" Immediately the tree withered.

When the disciples saw this, they were amazed. "How did the fig tree wither so quickly?" they asked.

Jesus replied, "Truly I tell you, if you have faith and do not doubt, not only can you do what was done to the fig tree, but also you can say to this mountain, 'Go, throw yourself into the sea,' and it will be done." Matthew 21:19–21

Jesus said that our words could uproot obstacles as well as cause things to wither. It is interesting that He said, "May you never bear fruit again!" And also, "[You can] do what was done to the fig tree."

We need to be very careful that we are not speaking withering words over ourselves or others. We need to speak fruitful words and have fruitful thoughts. When we speak negative things, it can cause our spiritual and creative gifts and lives to wither and no longer bear fruit.

God showed me that this is the condition of many people today. They have spoken negative or withering words over themselves, or have had negative or withering words spoken over them by someone else, which has caused their gifts and spiritual fruit to dry up. God is now giving us an opportunity to reverse this. We need to recognize areas of our lives that once flourished but are now withering. We can speak over these areas with prayers like, "Be fruitful and no longer wither!"

Getting Greater Authority

Our bodies are temples of the Holy Spirit. Note that just before Jesus withered the fig tree and talked about spiritual authority, He cleansed the temple in Jerusalem and drove out anything that was not of the Lord (Matthew 21:12–13). He then went on to heal the blind and the lame. This was a series of major prophetic acts that most people miss.

We can follow this pattern in our lives and see amazing results. We need to cleanse our temples by getting inner healing and repenting from anything that is contrary to

God's Word. This will allow us to open up spiritual blindness and get healed of being spiritually lame—not being able to see or walk in our destinies.

If you believe, you will receive whatever you ask for in prayer. Matthew 21:22

As we take care of these things, we will enter into a place of greater authority in prayer. This is going to be an amazing time that will align you with God's destiny. Do not be discouraged if it does not line up exactly on the calendar. God is full of grace, and we can step into His power for our lives at any point. As the books of Heaven are being reconciled, you can expect repayment for past seasons.

Reaping for All Your Weeping

Get ready to break out of the season you have been in and into something completely new. The Lord is gathering together those who have gone through difficult times and also the forerunners—those who have been set aside for this very time.

I will surely assemble all of you, O Jacob, I will surely gather the remnant of Israel; I will put them together like sheep of the fold, like a flock in the midst of their pasture; **they shall make a loud noise because of so many people.**

*The one who breaks open will come up before them; **they will break out**, pass through the gate, and go out by it; their king will pass before them, with the Lord at their head.* Micah 2:12–13 NKJV

The *loud noise* is a new sound coming in the spirit; as they gather, this new sound will break open the gates and restraints will fall off you. A *breakout* power and anointing is coming, and the Lord is going to open a new gate in the spirit. Those who have felt they are in prison or being held back are going to have a sudden prison-break experience.

Tears That Bring Change

Record my misery; list my tears on your scroll—are they not in your record? Psalm 56:8

A major shift in the spiritual atmosphere—for the good—is here. Many people have been crying out for change, justice, healing and relief from the struggles happening all over the world.

This has been a difficult season, and the Lord is now shifting the spiritual atmosphere as a result of your prayers and tears. The Lord has not forgotten your tears, and all of your prayers have been placed in a scroll or book in Heaven.

These books are now being reconciled, and this will bring the changes that we all have been crying out for. This will include financial repayment, injustices resolved, relationships healed and new clarity and vision for what God is calling you to.

Jesus Cried Too

During the days of Jesus' life on earth, he offered up prayers and petitions with fervent cries and tears to the one who could save him from death, and he was heard because of his reverent submission. Hebrews 5:7

The tears of the people who were weeping for the loss of Lazarus moved Jesus to tears, and He ultimately raised His friend from the dead. Tears can change the spiritual atmosphere and bring amazing miracles.

When Jesus saw her weeping, and the Jews who had come along with her also weeping, he was deeply moved in spirit and troubled. ... Jesus wept. John 11:33, 35

God is anointing our tears with greater power. In the past season, we could cry buckets of tears but not see results. This is now changing, and our weeping is turning into reaping. This is going to open up the heavens and release God's anointing to bring miracles in your life.

Outpouring of Blessing

How enriched are they who find their strength in the Lord;
within their hearts are the highways of holiness! Even when
their paths wind through the dark valley of tears, they dig deep
to find a pleasant pool where others find only pain. He gives to
them a brook of blessing filled from the rain of an outpouring.
Psalm 84:5–6 TPT

We are coming out of a season of the dark valley of tears, and God is using it to bring a brook of blessing. Watch for a highway of holiness to open before you. The Lord is going to bring you strength to overcome the things that have held you back in the past.

You will suddenly have new power to overcome what used to overcome you. A new breakout anointing that is going to sweep the world is coming for addictions. It will also bring a new release of deeper intimacy with the Lord that will allow you to experience love in greater ways.

Heavenly Encounter: Valley of Tears

I want to share with you another excerpt from my heavenly journal. This was an encounter I had on June 3, 2017. The Lord led me that morning to Psalm 84 in The Passion Translation. For the sake of space in this book, I am only going to share a few verses from Psalm 84 that apply to this particular spiritual encounter. I would encourage you to read the entire Psalm, especially in The Passion Translation, because it is so powerful.

As in other encounters, I began having detailed interactive visions after reading the verses the Lord had spoken to me. I was then invited into a place in the heavenly realm where I had this encounter. What I am about to read was spoken to me, but the Lord is speaking this to you as well.

[Beginning of Encounter]

Deep within me are these lovesick longings, desires and daydreams of living in union with you. When I'm near you my heart and my soul will sing and worship with my joyful songs of you, my true source and spring of life! Psalm 84:2 TPT

How enriched are they who find their strength in the Lord; within their hearts are the highways of holiness!

Even when their paths wind through the dark valley of tears, they dig deep to find a pleasant pool where others find only pain. He gives to them a brook of blessing filled from the rain of an outpouring. They grow stronger and stronger with every step forward, and the God of all gods will appear before them in Zion. Psalm 84:5–7 TPT

For just one day of intimacy with you is like a thousand days of joy rolled into one! I'd rather stand at the threshold in

front of the Gate Beautiful, ready to go in and worship my God, than to live my life without you in the most beautiful palace of the wicked.

For the Lord God is brighter than the brilliance of a sunrise! Wrapping himself around me like a shield, he is so generous with his gifts of grace and glory. Those who walk along his paths with integrity will never lack one thing they need, for he provides it all!

O Lord of Heaven's Armies, what euphoria fills those who forever trust in you! Psalm 84: 10–12 TPT

The Lord said, "I understand your lovesick longings, and I want you to know that I am near you all the time. I am watching over you and angels are assigned to you, singing songs and worshiping around you. I have heard your cries and your longings, and things are now being brought into place."

The Spring of Life

I met with the Lord in the house where I go visit Him daily in Heaven. My heart was heavy, and I had some serious concerns that I wanted to talk to the Lord about. I had been walking through a very difficult season, and needed to understand what was happening and what is yet to come. We were suddenly taken from the house, and we were then sitting by a flowing brook of water.

The Lord said, "I am the Spring of Life, and you can come and sit by this quiet place and it will restore your soul. You are coming out of the dark valley of tears. You have dug deeply into Me and have struck pools of living water that you are coming to each day. I am now sending you a brook of blessing. I am going to give you an outpouring in your life. But first, there are some things that need to be taken care of and brought into place. You are growing stronger and stronger with every step forward."

Then Jesus said, "Get up and let's take a walk because there is something I want to show you." I was so overwhelmed with all that I have been going through, and I was weeping the entire way. I cried bitterly because the road to get here has been so hard. I was battling with trying to stay positive and in faith, but I could no longer hide my emotions. I fell down a few times because my strength left me. Jesus picked me up and began to carry me to our destination.

The Gate Beautiful

We came to a very large gate; it was golden and had colorful inlay. I looked and there were now thousands of people gathering here. Some of them walked on their own. Others like me had to be carried because they were so weary. The name written on the gate was The Gate Beautiful. Jesus and the entire group were now standing in front of this gate.

Jesus said, "As you step inside this gate, you are stepping into your created purposes. Inside this gate are all the things I have promised you. It contains the longings of your heart and the reason you came into the world. Once you walk through this gate, you will no longer walk through the valley of tears."

The Valley of Tears

I looked back, and I could see that I had been walking through a dark season—through a winding road that led through the dark valley of tears. I looked around me and saw that many others were gathering at the entrance of The Gate Beautiful. It was not open yet, but we all knew this gate was about to open, and there was going to be a change coming for us all. We had great anticipation, our strength started to return and I was starting to feel hope again. The valley of tears had been long and difficult. Everyone gathering at the gate had walked through this valley. There were pools of water at the sides of the road, and I realized these were our tears that had filled them.

The Road of Righteousness

The Lord said, "Your valley of tears is now going to turn into a road of righteousness. Many people have walked this road, but they only focused on the pain. But you have dug deeply in My presence, and you have discovered My pleasant pools of living water in the midst of your dark times. You have all paved the way for others to come into this new season that is opening now. The road of righteousness is paved with tears."

We looked down, and the road we were standing on was made up of small crystals of our tears. I looked around and there were now many people gathering at the entrance to The Gate Beautiful. We had all walked through a difficult time to get here.

What Is inside the Gate?

I had not noticed before, but there was a very bright white light shining behind The Gate Beautiful. I could smell the fragrance of spring rain, flowers and growth.

The Lord said, "Inside this gate will be the greatest joy you have ever experienced. You will step into My perfect timing, and I will accomplish through you in one day what could take years without Me.

"Time will be on your side, and you will receive new understanding of My Kingdom. Inside this gate will be the start of the Great Revival. Satan has asked to take your lives, but you have all made it through the painful preparation and testing. You can stay here in My presence until the gate opens. You will be safe, and your strength will continue to increase. Your time of preparation is now here."

Shields of Faith

Then angels came and brought us new shields that had the word *Faith* written on them. As the shields were handed to us, they wrapped around our bodies and fitted us like futuristic armor. It reminded me of the movie *Iron Man*.

I was handed my shield of faith, and it wrapped around my entire body like liquid, covering me from head to toe. I felt safer now than I did before. I was feeling very vulnerable, as I am a man of love and peace walking through a fierce battle around me.

Wait Here

The Lord said, "You will need to wait here in My presence in front of The Gate Beautiful. It is going to open very soon, and you will cross over into the new season and the start of all that I have been showing you. It will not be long." Then Jesus flashed us a smile, and I came out of the encounter.

[End of Encounter]

This is happening right now! The Lord is opening The Gate Beautiful, and this is going to allow you access to all that you will need to step into your created purpose. If you have felt tired and weary, if you have wept and not seen answers, if you feel like you are not moving forward ... it is because you are with many others who are experiencing the same thing. We are all coming out of the valley of tears; we are coming out of the wilderness and waiting on the Lord to open the door to the new season.

CHAPTER 8

MYSTERIES REVEALED FROM HEAVEN

I want to share with you one of the more powerful encounters I had in my 50 days behind the veil of Heaven. It came in a narrative form, which is unlike anything I have ever done with my own writing style and it was a supernatural download that I received.

This encounter happened on May 9, 2017. If you have read previous encounters in this book, then there is no need to explain how it comes to me and how these things work. I will jump right into the action.

[Beginning of Encounter]

I Went into My House in Heaven

There does not seem to be a lot of activity going on, because it is a day of rest. I heard the Lord say, "I'm going to take you into deeper understanding of My rest."

I began to walk with the Lord. The Lord and I walked for quite some distance through a beautiful place with gardens and still water. As we walked by, it was as if some things were living. There was a brook that sang songs, flowers that would spin and dance, and the colors were very rich and deep. What I noticed most was the peace and rest. Everything seemed easy and light walking next to the Lord. We sat down next to the still waters, and they began to refresh my soul.

Sitting by the Still Waters

I began to weep because I realized how much striving I had done in my life. The Lord laid His hand on me and said, "Don't cry, because things are about to change for you. There is a season to work and a season to rest; a season to battle and a season of peace. I'm going to show you how to walk at peace in the midst of all seasons. No matter what is going on around you, you will be able to rest in the storm like I did in Matthew 8."

At that, I was taken to the scene from Matthew 8:24 where the disciples were in the boat in a furious storm. It came without warning, but Jesus was sleeping. He got up and rebuked the storm, and the winds and waves calmed down completely.

Jesus said to me, "Once you understand the harmony and flow of Heaven, and the authority that I have given you, you can ask whatever you wish and it will be done."

Then He touched me, and I felt my storm calm. My body was not feeling good until He touched me. Things began to change inside physically—even emotionally and spiritually. I suddenly had greater understanding.

The Map of Times, Seasons and Places

I was seeing the scenes from Matthew 8, where Jesus knew when to go to the other side of the lake and remove the demonic stronghold that was keeping people from passing by (Matthew 8:28). Not only did Jesus go there to drive out the demons from these men, but He also opened an access point in the spirit for His purposes. These two men had come into agreement with Legion and were holding down something in that land. They were demonic gatekeepers over that region.

The Lord said, "I want to give you [He was talking about everyone, not just me] understanding of times and seasons, and discernment of the demonic strongholds that are stopping people from coming to Me." Then I saw a map open in Jesus' lap. It was like many of the other things I have seen in Heaven, both ancient-looking and high-tech at the same time. The map seemed to have a 3-D look with lights on various places.

Jesus took my hand and placed it over one of these lights on the map in His lap. Something lit up like a 3-D hologram. It showed details, timing and wisdom on how to remove the demonic strongholds over that place.

Then I realized it was not just places. Some of these lights were people, some were churches, some were businesses, some were cities and regions, but they all had one thing in common: They were gateways into the deeper things of Heaven. The enemy had encamped and set up what looked like strongholds over these places and people.

The Mystery of Regions and the Calling of Matthew

I sat for quite some time next to Jesus with this map in His lap. I was so fascinated and fixed on it because I have never seen anything like it. There was a mystery of God's timing for all things. Just as Jesus calmed the storm and then drove out Legion, it opened up the calling of Matthew. I asked the Lord, "What did driving out Legion have to do with the calling of Matthew?" In Matthew 8, Jesus drives out Legion and opens up the region; then in Matthew 9 was the calling of Matthew.

Jesus said, "Matthew was a forerunner of the Joseph Anointing, as he had been a gateway to controlling finances. Satan had set up a stronghold over him, but I stepped in and redeemed him and his calling.

"Some demonic gateways and strongholds are more apparent, like that of Legion, which was controlling the entire region with fear. Others, like Matthew, were political and financial, and the demonic was not quite as apparent. But as I released him, it opened up the heavens for the new wineskin that was coming." I knew Jesus was talking about the Matthew 9 wineskin message He brought that day.

Strategy to Change People and Places

While Jesus was having dinner at Matthew's house, many tax collectors and sinners came and ate with him and his disciples. When the Pharisees saw this, they asked his disciples, "Why does your teacher eat with tax collectors and sinners?" On hearing this, Jesus said, "It is not the healthy who need a doctor, but the sick. But go and learn what this means: 'I desire mercy, not sacrifice' [this was from Hosea 6:6]. *For I have not come to call the righteous, but sinners."* Matthew 9:10–13

It was as if I was sitting in the room during Matthew 9, and I was watching this happen as Jesus recounted it to me. Then it all made sense to me: Jesus had to bring down a political stronghold that was over Matthew and his friends. Something happened that day in the spiritual realm. Not only was Matthew converted and his gifts redeemed, but it also opened something in the spiritual realm to bring the new wineskin mentioned in Matthew 9:17. I was marveling at the depth of this mystery.

New Wineskin Coming

Jesus looked at me and said, "For you have not come to call the righteous, but the sinners. Matthew was considered an abomination. This is the new wineskin that I am bringing.

"Many of my people have focused on ministering to the righteous and have neglected the sinners—those who are considered an abomination and even untouchable. They have neglected those of different political and belief systems.

"But I tell you, I have come for all people. I healed those with leprosy who were considered untouchable. I healed the servant of the Roman centurion. I healed the demon–possessed men, and I healed and called Matthew. This was all my Father's will, as I only did what I saw the Father doing."

Jesus' stature seemed to change. He was now speaking to me in greater authority, almost as if His words and eyes were imparting something that was needed.

Then He said, "This is why I had to bring a new wineskin for the new wine of My presence. This is why I will indeed do it again. You will need to pour this new wine into a new wineskin, for surely it will burst the old. The coming Great Revival will not fit into the old-wineskin churches."

Mystery of God's Timing

As I sat with Jesus, all these things were coming alive from Matthew 8–9, and I was given greater understanding of God's timing and great love for people. I knew this had to do with the mystery of God's timing that I had heard in Heaven several times before.

I was still sitting next to Jesus, and He still had the map in His lap. But now He leaned against me and pulled me close to His chest. My heart became one with His, and I could feel the heartbeat of Heaven. God's timing became mine, and I knew this was going to be imparted to others.

Jesus folded up the map like a scroll, and it was placed inside me. He said, "You will need this to walk in My presence and timing. I tell you, when you get in time with Heaven, everything will flow. You will know where to go, who to talk to and the words to say that will bring the Kingdom on Earth. For this is an impartation of 'on Earth as it is in Heaven.'"

As I sat there with Jesus during this Matthew 8–9 encounter, I felt like I could stay in this place and everything seemed to make sense. But then the Lord got up and began to walk. In the distance, I saw a place where we were going. He began to walk briskly ahead of me, and I had to speed up to catch up to Him.

Going to See Melchizedek

I asked Jesus, "Where are we going now?" He said to me, "We are going to go meet Melchizedek, the high priest."

Suddenly Hebrews 7–8 came alive, and I saw in the distance what looked like a tabernacle. As we got closer, I could hear a glorious chorus singing praises to the Lord. It was a low-pitched sound, lower than the sound of our songs on Earth, and I did not quite understand the language that was being sung.

But then Jesus turned and touched my ears, and I could understand the song. It was from Hebrews 7:17, "*... You are a priest forever, in the order of Melchizedek.*"

Melchizedek and Matthew Connection

As we were walking, Jesus said to me, "You must understand the connection between Matthew and Melchizedek."

Now the law requires that the descendants of Levi who become priests to collect a tenth from the people ... Hebrews 7:5a

Matthew's name was Levi. He had a calling in his genealogy that gave him authority from Heaven to collect money, but he was using it to control people. This is similar to what is happening in the Church today. Matthew's gift was redeemed, and he stepped into his true calling. There is a connection with Matthew, Melchizedek and the men and women who carry a Joseph Anointing.

Jesus said, "When I called Matthew, he was sitting in a tollbooth collecting taxes. He was a financial gatekeeper, but not in the right spirit. Melchizedek was also a financial gatekeeper that released a blessing over Abraham and his descendants. One of Abraham's descendants was Joseph, who picked up the financial calling and blessing. He became a gatekeeper over Israel and released blessings during the time of the famine in Egypt. Every generation has financial gatekeepers to bring about the work of the Kingdom from Heaven to Earth."

Ordination of the Joseph People

I wanted to sit here and process all of this, as it was really heavy and deep. But Jesus seemed to be in a hurry, as if there was a timing issue involved in where we were going. As we approached the tabernacle, it became very bright and joyous. There was a special ceremony going on inside, and there was a very long line of people waiting to get in. We bypassed the line, and went directly in. I was now standing and observing people being ordained into the order of Melchizedek. I have never understood this, but now revelation is opening up. His name means "King of Righteousness; King of Peace."

As we went into the tabernacle, I saw a blazing altar at the front. There were cherubim singing this song, *"You are a priest forever, in the order of Melchizedek"* (Hebrews 7:17b). I looked and saw that those who were being ordained into the order of Melchizedek were not actually being ordained by Melchizedek himself. Instead, there were priests who had been given authority from Heaven to ordain these people.

I knew it was not like a priest on Earth, but it was someone who would walk in priestly anointing and authority like Abraham. As those in line to be ordained approached, they would stop at a place in the front, before the blazing altar. They would hold up their arms to Heaven and tilt their head back and one of the priests would take what looked like a golden ladle and scoop liquid fire from the altar and pour it into their mouth.

As they did this, the countenance of those being ordained changed and there was a fire placed in their belly. They were given a greater authority to walk in the spirit.

At first, I did not understand who these people were. Then I realized that many of these were the Joseph Anointing people—those who would become gatekeepers of Kingdom finances on Earth because there had been negative gatekeepers controlling the money for the new things that are coming. There were both men and women being ordained.

I could see that the line stretched for what looked like eternity. The next one would step up, and the same thing would happen, and the cherubim would sing. Then they would exit the doors to the right and left which were full of bright white light. I knew these doors brought them back to Earth. These were living people who were getting this ordination and impartation of God's fire and authority. They were bringing it back with them to Earth.

The Office of Melchizedek

I stood and watched this go on for quite some time. Then Jesus grabbed my hand and took me behind the altar and through a long corridor until we reached the office of Melchizedek. I guess I had not realized that he still had an office in Heaven.

As we entered a golden door to his office, I was expecting something different. It did not look like an office on Earth, but the walls were full of living testimonies. These were like holograms—family crests, shields, all different types of things on the walls—that were speaking the testimony of the Lord. When someone got close to them, their audible voices sang out the testimonies over that person. It was a harmony like nothing I've heard before.

My spirit man was strengthened as I heard these testimonies. I was in awe of all that the Lord had done for people. Melchizedek was sitting in a golden chair, like one with authority. He was given authority in Heaven for all that he had done on Earth. I was feeling so overwhelmed by God's presence that I almost fell down. But two angels came, one on each side, and held me up.

Counsel Room of Heaven

I'm now understanding that this is a Counsel Room in Heaven. It is a courtroom, but it does not look like the courtrooms on Earth or the ones that I had pictured or even been part of. Melchizedek was a judge and priest, and there were several chairs placed around him in a semicircle. People would come in and sit, and he would make decisions based on their request. I suddenly realized that these were the tough cases, involving those who had been held down by the enemy and for those who had high callings.

In Front of Melchizedek

The two angels placed me in a seat in front of Melchizedek. He said to me, "Do not be afraid, for the Lord is with you." I was wondering what I was going to say, or what I was supposed to do. But suddenly the testimonies on the wall began to cry out loudly—all the testimonies on Earth that defended my case.

I heard things like, "This man has been treated unjustly. He is a servant of the Most High God ..." Others were crying out the testimonies of people on Earth who have been blessed and touched by my ministry. And yet others were talking about the things that I have yet to do for the Kingdom, and the reason I had come to Earth was being spoken over me.

Melchizedek raised his right hand as if to quiet the testimonies, and they were suddenly silent. I was sitting there in front of him. He had compassion in his eyes, and he said with authority, "This one has been treated unjustly and overlooked for too long. Son, the Lord is with you, and He has kept you alive for this very time. You have asked to raise up a generation of people that were neglected and forgotten. The Lord has heard your prayers, and now the Books of Heaven are open over you." I knew he was talking about the Billion Soul Revival and the outcasts.

Golden Book Opened

At that, I saw a vision of a golden book open over me. It was as if it was opened over the entire room. From that book flowed everything needed to fulfill my calling. Then Melchizedek said, "Stand him up," for my strength had left me, and I could not stand on my own in this room. The two angels came and grabbed my arms, stood me up and held me in place. Melchizedek came down a few steps and stood in front of me. He placed his hand on my heart, and another one on my head, and I felt power and authority flow into me. It was like a colorful electricity.

Room for Those Who Are Ready

The experience was so powerful, and the presence of God was so strong, that I "went out" in the spirit. I came to in a recovery room called Those Who Are Ready. In that room, I was being equipped with things I would need. New armor was placed on me, angels were being assigned to me and strategies were being imparted.

I was not alone in this room, as there were many people who are now stepping into this new season and have gone through the tests. These are the ones who survived "the great testing that comes before The Great Revival."

Shower of God's Presence

In front of me are others ready to go out this door. I see what looks like a shower with water of the Spirit washing over each person that goes through the door. I heard the Lord say, "This is the washing of My Word, for My Blood has made you clean. But now receive the refreshing of the Holy Spirit."

At that, I went through the shower of God's presence, and it felt so good I stopped and stood there for a while as it washed over me. Then I felt a push on my back that forced me through the door of blinding white light.

[End of Encounter]

I want to encourage you that, even though these things happened to me, there were so many people from all walks of life receiving these blessings. I want to share it with you to encourage you to receive these by faith for yourself. The Lord is calling you to a new level, and He is imparting strategies from Heaven to you right now as you read this. This is not only for prophets or leaders; it is for all those who cry out to the Lord for more!

CHAPTER 9

CLOSING ENCOURAGEMENT

I want to encourage you to read through this book again, and ask the Lord to open up revelation and deeper understanding to you. The Lord spoke to me that those who read the heavenly journal encounters would begin to have encounters of their own. They might not be the same level as what I had, but God is now visiting people through dreams, visions and speaking through the Bible.

Strategic Season of Dreams

Watch for dreams and night visitations, as higher-level revelation is going to start pouring out to you. In some cases, you might not remember these types of dreams or visitations. The reason for this is that God can reveal it to you in a way that will hide it from the enemy. This is a strategy that God uses, but many people are not aware of it. They can come in a form of a dream that you know you had but cannot remember. Or you wake up feeling like something significant happened.

During the night the mystery was revealed to Daniel in a vision. Then Daniel praised the God of heaven and said: "Praise be to the name of God for ever and ever; wisdom and power are his. He changes times and seasons; he deposes kings and raises up others. He gives wisdom to the wise and knowledge to the discerning. He reveals deep and hidden things; he knows what lies in darkness, and light dwells with him." Daniel 2:19–22

God is releasing wisdom and power, and He is concealing strategies and revelation for your future. This will help hide your promotion and plans from the enemy, and bring you less warfare. Times and seasons are changing quickly, so be aware that the way you currently do things might not work in the new season that is now upon us. The Lord is releasing deep and hidden things, and He is going to reveal the plans of the enemy against you and bring them into the light.

Prophetic Dream of a Revival Museum

[Beginning of Dream]

I had a prophetic dream that the late leader and founder of the Vineyard Christian Fellowship movement, John Wimber, was giving a lecture about previous moves of God and what stopped them. He had a museum that allowed you to experience the moves and revivals of God. It was very interactive and demonstrated each move of God, and allowed you to interact with it.

I walked up to an exhibit, and it was the life of Elvis Presley. Elvis had a call of God on his life and music. He used it the wrong way, and it never came about as God intended. In this interactive display, his calling died like a plane crash. You could run various scenarios on a computer to see how things would have been different. I ran it in dozens of ways, but his plane crashed every time. This did not mean that he died in a plane crash; it was symbolic of the crash of his calling and anointing that had come from the Lord.

Next, I saw a large statue that had a clock on it. It was lying on the ground, broken into pieces. It was a move of God too, and an angel told me this represented the various moves of God *over time* that had gotten destroyed. There were things that looked like dinosaurs in this display. I knew that meant the old religious spirit had stopped these moves of God.

Then I saw a very large exhibit that was pouring rain inside, but the rain stopped at the edge of the exhibit. It was amazing. I stepped inside and got drenched, and warm wind was blowing. As I walked through the exhibit, I came to an ocean I knew was on the West Coast of the United States. There was a breaker wall holding the waves back. I climbed the wall to see the waves, and realized that this wall was about to give way and the waves were going to crash into the land. I turned and saw the prophet Paul Cain in a pulpit, preaching about the moves of God.

An angel said, "This is the latter rain movement that is yet to come, as the prophet Paul Cain had prophesied. This movement is going to come, and it will bring with it the power and anointing greater than previous moves of the Lord. The wave of the Holy Spirit is about to crest over the breaker walls, and it is going to flow to the world.

[End of Dream]

God is going to give us revelation about what stopped and derailed previous revivals, and how we can work with Him to bring one of the greatest moves of God to Earth.

Dream: Musical Chairs at 57,000 Feet

Throughout the Bible, we see times of transition into new seasons. With every new season comes new leaders and new wisdom for how to operate in this new time. What used to work in the old season is not effective for the new. We are in a time of transition, and a major season of change is upon us.

He changes times and seasons; he deposes kings and raises up others. He gives wisdom to the wise and knowledge to the discerning. Daniel 2:21

I had a significant dream some years ago, and the Lord spoke to me that this dream is for now.

[Beginning of Dream]

In the dream, I was in a room with many leaders. A tornado was approaching fast, and there was no time to react. The tornado entered the room, and everything began to rotate clockwise. I saw a chair floating by as I, too, was being picked up and floating as well. I was about to grab hold of the chair when the Lord spoke audibly to everyone in the room, "Many people have died because they have held onto their chair."

Just then I heard the cry of a leader being swept away because he was hanging onto his chair. Then I heard a voice and a song on the radio say, "There are musical chairs at 57,000 feet."

[End of Dream]

The Meaning of the Dream

There is a change coming in the Kingdom of God and in those who occupy certain positions. In order for us to be more easily used by the Lord, we must hold our current positions loosely, and allow God to position us. The tornado was allowed by God (a clockwise spin, as opposed to counter-clockwise). In dreams, chairs often represent our position. Those who try to hold onto a position, instead of flowing in what God has, will not be able to survive the change that is coming.

To interpret the meaning of the number 57,000: 5+7=12. Twelve is the number of leadership and government. The fact that the number was in the tens of thousands indicates a higher level or degree of change in leadership. As these changes come about, there will be a shift in the entire Church and government. New positions will open that have been occupied by people who are not necessarily called to be doing what they are doing.

Some leaders and people who have lost their vision will gain fresh new insight from the Lord and begin leading their churches to a new level. Others will need to step aside and allow different people to lead. The Lord spoke to me that this is coming, and we are called to help bring about one of the greatest changes we have seen in history.

Prophecy of Three Kings

As God begins to move and bring the new paradigm or wineskin for the new revival, do not be surprised if not everyone is able to receive it. This is actually common, as people and leaders from previous moves of God often reject the new thing when God brings it.

An example of this is with King Saul and King David. God called King Saul, and there was a point where the season changed and the anointing and calling fell upon David. Their leadership styles were totally different, and God used David to birth a new level of wisdom that had never been seen before on Earth through his son, Solomon. I heard Larry Randolph talk about this in the past. Prophetically, we can view these three kings who are similar to three moves of God that have happened over the past 100 years.

King Saul represents the old, more rigid and structured religion. This worked during that season, but later they lost track of loving people.

King David, the man after God's own heart—the man of love, but also of war—came on the scene. David represents the Charismatic movement that loves God and worships freely. But like David, many of us were guilty of bloodshed by wounding others. David was not permitted by God to build the temple because of this.

At a young age, King Solomon brought a level of wisdom that had never been seen on Earth. Solomon was able to build the temple because of God's love and promises to David. This is a prophetic sign of what is coming to us now.

The Lord is going to move on a younger generation in a revival that will impact the entire world. God is going to raise up a new level of leadership on a young generation that is going to move in worldwide favor and blessing. This does not mean that the rest of us have no part of it. God is a family—the fact that He is Father, Son and Holy Spirit shows this. We are all being invited to be part of what God is bringing.

The Heavenly Adjustment Department

In order to bring about revival, there has to be a change in those who have been leading, but not using the gifts and assignments they carry. Because many people have rejected the revivals the Lord has wanted to bring, Heaven has needed to make adjustments. Every time someone says "no" to a calling of the Lord, it takes time for those things to realign and the assignments to get to others. This is also why it may seem that the things God has promised you have been delayed.

This has been going on for the past two decades or more, and there have been some changes in many people's callings. New assignments were released from the Heavenly Adjustment Department. This will be the start of some major realignments and reassignments coming over the next few years. The important thing is for you to keep your eyes on the Lord.

Peace I leave with you; my peace I give you. I do not give to you as the world gives. Do not let your hearts be troubled and do not be afraid. ... I have told you now before it happens, so that when it does happen you will believe. John 14:27, 29

My prayer for you is that you would be able to receive the Lord's words in this book, and that it will bring peace and rest to you in the midst of the storms. I pray that you would be able to rise above the attacks of the enemy, and be confident that the Lord loves you. He has prepared a way for you, and a door in the spirit is now opening for you. Everything will begin to fall into place once you walk through this door. Yes, we will still have trials and challenges, but the Lord is releasing us into a new level of His power and love that will make it all worthwhile.

And now these three remain: faith, hope and love. But the greatest of these is love. 1 Corinthians 13:13

I want to commission you to be God's hope and love to people everywhere. We can shift the negative spiritual atmosphere that has been dominant. Greater is the One in you than the one in the world. Together we can reach the world with the love of Jesus Christ.

ABOUT DOUG

Doug Addison is the founder and President of InLight Connection. Doug is a prophetic speaker, author and coach. He is best known for his *Daily Prophetic Words, Spirit Connection* webcast, podcast and blog.

Doug's message of love, hope and acceptance reaches people around the world! His powerful, lighthearted style of teaching and coaching helps open people to discover their spiritual identity and personal destiny as they experience God's supernatural love and power. He and his wife Linda live in Los Angeles, California where they are impacting the arts and entertainment and media industries.

DougAddison.com

RESOURCES FROM DOUG ADDISON

Prophetic Forecast, Volume 1

In the *Prophetic Forecast, Volume 1 (2016)*, Doug Addison shares the prophetic words, dreams and supernatural encounters he has received from God in 2016 for what God is doing over the next 7 years—and puts them together into one easy-to-read book for you.

This book is a tool to help you align your life with what God is doing. You will get to know God's heart better as you understand these prophetic insights.

Prophetic Forecast, Volume 2

In the *Prophetic Forecast, Volume 2 (2017)*, Doug Addison shares revelation he received regarding the coming revival.

Describing the details of several encounters he had with God and messages he received during the *Days of Awe* (the time period between Rosh Hashanah and Yom Kippur), Doug opens new understanding about what we can expect in the coming years.

Discovering the Supernatural

This book draws from Doug Addison's personal journey and shares stories of his heavenly encounters with God and the angelic realm.

In *Discovering the Supernatural: Interacting with the Angelic & Heavenly Realms in Your Daily Life*, you will get an insider account as Doug addresses the questions he had along the way and answers questions others have asked him as they have learned to hear God and understand the supernatural.

Unlocking Your Breakthrough Self-Coaching Toolkit

The *Unlocking Your Breakthrough Self-Coaching Toolkit* is a result of Doug's 25+ years of coaching himself and others to successfully reach goals. The strategies and tools in this toolkit could be exactly what you need to break through and finally step into your dreams!

You will be getting everything you need to go through the process of discovering your life purpose, creating a manageable action plan for your goals and coaching yourself through any obstacles you face as you go after your destiny. When you receive the *Unlocking Your Breakthrough Self-Coaching Toolkit* you will get the practical strategies and tools you need to finally reach your goals.

How to Flip Your Financial Future

This book packs a powerful punch to activate you in practical Kingdom strategies for sowing and reaping, getting out of debt, increasing your income and even starting or growing your business or ministry, so you can *flip* your financial future ... and flip it good!

God Spoke, Now What?

God is continually speaking to you—sending you messages to help you as you walk through your life journey. Oftentimes, people do not realize when God is speaking to them, and they do not know how to interpret and activate the messages they receive.

In his book, *God Spoke, Now What? Activating Your Prophetic Word*, Doug Addison not only shows you how to recognize the messages God is sending you through dreams, life experiences, the media, other people or natural circumstances; he also teaches you how to interpret the messages and activate them so you can see breakthroughs happen in your life.

Write Your Book Now!

Write Your Book Now! is a self-guided online course with everything you need to get your book written and published as quickly as possible—without sacrificing quality. Writing a book used to be a long, painful task, but *Write Your Book Now!* helps you accelerate the writing process so you can have a completed manuscript—in as little as 30 days!

Write a Book Quickly: Unlock Your Creative Spirit

Whether you are just starting out or are an experienced writer, this precise book can help you get to a new level. Tap into your creative nature, learn secrets of writing, publishing tips, writing resources, exercises and more.

Spiritual Identity Theft Exposed

The rise of identity theft in the world today parallels what is happening spiritually to people everywhere. People have been blinded to their true identity and the destiny they were created to live. *Spiritual Identity Theft Exposed* contains seven strategies from darkness and seven remedies to change your life forever.

Understand Your Dreams Now: Spiritual Dream Interpretation

Doug Addison's *Understand Your Dreams Now: Spiritual Dream Interpretation,* is drawn from decades of classroom and real-world experiences. This book contains everything you need to get started or to go to a new level of interpreting dreams. Includes a 300-symbol dream dictionary.

Dream Crash Course

Understanding dreams does not have to be difficult! Doug Addison is an expert dream interpreter who has interpreted over 25,000 dreams and has trained thousands of dream interpreters worldwide. He has developed a crash course on how to understand your dreams quickly.

This is everything you need in one online program. This course includes ten online videos, mp3s, study guide, dream journal, symbols dictionary and more!

Prophetic Tattoo and Piercing Interpretation

Now you can learn the inside secrets to *Prophetic Tattoo and Piercing Interpretation* from Doug Addison. After years of development, Doug Addison is making this one–of–a–kind online training available to you. Find what you need to get started in this new cutting-edge outreach strategy!

This online training includes seven online videos, mp3s, study guide, tattoo reference cards and more.

Visit: DougAddison.store

Made in the USA
Columbia, SC
31 January 2018